THOMAS (TENNESSEE) WILLIAMS

THE GLASS
MENAGERIE

NOTES

COLES EDITORIAL BOARD

Bound to stay open

Publisher's Note

Otabind (Ota-bind). This book has been bound using the patented Otabind process. You can open this book at any page, gently run your finger down the spine, and the pages will lie flat.

P9-DGB-357

ABOUT COLES NOTES

COLES NOTES have been an indispensible aid to students on five continents since 1948.

COLES NOTES are available for a wide range of individual literary works. Clear, concise explanations and insights are provided along with interesting interpretations and evaluations.

Proper use of COLES NOTES will allow the student to pay greater attention to lectures and spend less time taking notes. This will result in a broader understanding of the work being studied and will free the student for increased participation in discussions.

COLES NOTES are an invaluable aid for review and exam preparation as well as an invitation to explore different interpretive paths.

COLES NOTES are written by experts in their fields. It should be noted that any literary judgement expressed herein is just that – the judgement of one school of thought. Interpretations that diverge from, or totally disagree with any criticism may be equally valid.

COLES NOTES are designed to supplement the text and are not intended as a substitute for reading the text itself. Use of the NOTES will serve not only to clarify the work being studied, but should enhance the readers enjoyment of the topic.

ISBN 0-7740-3029-1

© COPYRIGHT 1998 AND PUBLISHED BY
COLES PUBLISHING COMPANY
TORONTO - CANADA
PRINTED IN CANADA

Manufactured by Webcom Limited
Cover finish: Webcom's Exclusive **DURACOAT**

CONTENTS

Thomas (Tennessee) Williams
Life and Works

Thomas Lanier Williams was born on March 26, 1911. The name Tennessee is a pseudonym he adopted years later, and for the taking of which he has offered a variety of reasons: that he found his given name too formidable; that early writing under his real name had been poor and had compromised him so that he needed to start anew with a fresh name; and that the pseudonym was meant to honor his forebears who had fought Indians in Tennessee.

Early Life and Education

It was in Mississippi, however, that Tennessee Williams was born. His maternal grandfather was an Episcopal minister in the Mississippi town of Columbus, and it was there that Williams and his sister, Rose, were raised. Their father, a travelling salesman for The International Shoe Company, was often away from home, and their childhood was further marred by frequent illnesses. Williams' sister, who is thought to be the model for many of the playwright's disturbed and withdrawn heroines, was slightly crippled and became a recluse. But for Williams, childhood sickness had one beneficial result: it provided him with abundant time for reading.

When Tennessee was about twelve, the family moved to St. Louis, Missouri, where the rows of brick houses seemed to him to be the color of "dried blood and mustard." The South began to take on mythic proportions to Williams even then. But it was in St. Louis that Williams began to write, and he published his first literary endeavor, a short story, which was published in *Weird Tales* magazine in 1928. The following year he entered the University of Missouri, bent upon a writing career. He was an exceedingly shy youth, and took to drinking to counteract his shyness. He failed ROTC. He was more successful in the realm of writing and won a number of small prizes for both prose and poetry.

Early Career as a Writer

In 1931, financial pressures and poor grades made it necessary for Williams to leave the university. He spent the next two years working for a shoe company. "The two years I spent were indescribable to me as an individual but of immense value to me as a writer," he says, "for they gave me first-hand knowledge of what it means to be a small wage-earner in a hopelessly routine job." His days passed in the warehouse, but at night he continued his efforts at writing. He would come home from work, drink innumerable cups of black coffee so that he could remain awake, and go to his room, where he turned out poems and stories. The frustrations of this type of day and night routine finally led to a nervous breakdown. Coming home from work one evening, Williams collapsed physically and was put in a hospital. Several weeks later he went to live with his grandparents in Memphis to recover his health.

Williams' Development as a Playwright

In 1936, his grandparents financed his return to college, this time at Washington University in St. Louis, where he again distinguished himself at writing. He won first prize in a play contest and went on to write for the Mummers, a well-known little theater group in Missouri. His first work for them was written in response to the director's call for an antimilitaristic play to share the program with Irwin Shaw's *Bury the Dead.* Williams wrote a farce called *Cairo, Shanghai, Bombay,* and his playwrighting career was launched. Two of his other scripts — *Candles in the Sun* and *Fugitive Kind*—were produced by the Mummers.

In 1937, Williams left Washington University to enrol at the university in Iowa City. Here, he helped pay his way by working in the Iowa State Hospital cafeteria, tutoring freshmen in English, and selling tickets for university plays. Here, too, he participated in a playwriting seminar, where he polished his theatrical skills, and was finally granted his Bachelor of Arts degree. From Iowa, Williams went to Chicago, where he tried to join the Works Progress Administration Writer's Project but in this attempt he was unsuccessful. "I still had, in those days," he says, "a touch of refinement in my social behavior which made me seem frivolous and decadent to the conscientiously rough-hewn pillars of the Chicago Project."

Leaving Chicago, Williams went back to his home in St. Louis, where he wrote his fourth long play, *Not About Nightingales.* This play was based on a newspaper item Williams had read that described the roasting alive of a group of rebellious prison convicts sent for correction to a hot room called "the Klondike." It was Williams' most macabre play. Years later he wrote: "I have never written anything since then that could compete with it in violence and horror."

During the winter of 1938-39, Williams lived in the French quarter in New Orleans (the neighborhood so beautifully rendered in *A Streetcar Named Desire*). In New Orleans he made another attempt to join the Writer's Project, and was again unsuccessful. He went to work as a waiter in a restaurant that featured twenty-five-cent meals. He worked during the day and wrote at night. He walked the streets of the quarter and became familiar with the colorful characters of the old city. For the first time in his life, he found himself sharing a sense of loneliness with people he had never known in St. Louis: prostitutes and bums, sailors and tramps, rootless poets and gamblers. In later years Williams recalled these people: "There was a sampling of all who were too brave or too frightened, too pure or too corrupt, too angry or too gentle, too clear or too confused, to accept the peace and comfort of respectability."

Early Recognition and First Production

In the summer of 1939, Williams worked as a ranch-hand on a pigeon farm in California. His job was to feed, water and pluck the squabs. He also worked with Clark's Bootery in Culver City, near the Metro-Goldwyn-Mayer Studios. He could not support himself with his writing, but little by little he began to gather a roster of significant accomplishments. He won the Group Theater Prize for his one-act sketches, *American Blues.* The citation from the Group Theater read, "To Tennessee Williams, twenty-four-years-old, of New Orleans, for *American Blues,* a group of three sketches which constitute a full-length play." Actually, Williams was twenty-eight when he won this award. It has only been in the last few years that he has admitted his age. Besides winning the Group Theater award, Williams won a $1,000 Rockefeller Grant to enable him to continue writing plays, and in 1940 a play of his had a major production—The Theater Guild produced his play, *Battle of Angels,* in Boston. Unfortunately, the play, which dealt with a wandering young writer and a sexually frustrated woman, was a failure and was withdrawn from performance. The somewhat lurid presentation of sex and adultery set in a southern locale shocked the Boston audience. The drama critic of the Boston *Globe* described the play as ". . . one of the most incredible dramas ever presented in Boston." Referring to the failure of the play, Williams said: "You can't mix up sex and religion as I did." He had never heard of an audience getting so angry with a play. On the opening night there were hisses of indignation as most of the audience departed in haste. Over a period of years, Williams rewrote *Angels* under the title, *Orpheus Descending,* which opened on Broadway in 1957, and as a screenplay for the motion picture, *The Fugitive Kind,* which appeared in 1960.

Second World War Years

After the failure of *Battle of Angels,* Williams continued to wander about the country, working at odd jobs and turning out stories and poems. In 1941, while in New Orleans, he heard the news of America's entry into the Second World War and reported for an army induction examination. He was classified 4F on physical grounds. Later he went to work for the U.S. Engineers in Jacksonville, Florida, as a teletype operator. In January of 1942, Williams went to New York, taking with him two plays he had completed in New Orleans. One of them, *I Rise in Flame, Cried the Phoenix,* was based on the final moments of D. H. Lawrence's life. This play, which was produced off-Broadway in April, 1959, is one of Williams' finest short plays. The second play, called *Stairs to the Roof,* had been started in 1940. It is a fantasy, sub-titled *A Prayer for the Wild of Heart that are kept in Cages.* It was based on Williams' experiences in the International Shoe Company. While *Stairs to the Roof* possesses an intensity of feeling that is characteristic of the best of Williams' work, it is not one of his better plays. It received its only production by a small theater group in Pasadena, California. In New York, Williams began a new play with a friend, Donald Windham. Together they developed a short story by D. H. Lawrence into a full-length play called *You Touched Me*. After completing the first draft of this play, Williams resumed his old habit of wandering. He went to Florida, where he completed a short play called *Ten Blocks on the Camino Real*, which was later turned into the three-act drama, *Camino Real*. Williams had his Rockefeller Grant renewed, and later obtained the American Academy of Arts and Letters Award for $1,000. Thus, he continued to live, supporting himself by a combination of literary grants and miscellaneous occupations until 1944, when *The Glass Menagerie* was produced in Chicago.

Success

The Glass Menagerie was an immediate success. Sensitive and original, it is to this day one of Williams' finest plays. It was produced in New York in 1945 and Williams' fame was established overnight. So successful was *The Glass Menagerie* that Williams was constantly courted by theater enthusiasts, producers, and actors. He began to lead a life that was entirely different from his former one. He moved out of the precarious tenancy of a furnished room and into an expensive eastside hotel. He dined on room service, and friends helped him with his wardrobe by selecting expensive suits. He did not want for money or encouragement, the very things which he had always desired. "The sort of life which I had had previous to this popular success," Williams said, "was one that required endurance, a life of clawing and scratching along a sheer surface and holding on tight with raw fingers to every inch of rock higher than the one caught hold of before. . . . I was not aware of how much vital energy had gone into this struggle until the struggle was removed. I was out on a level plateau with my arms still thrashing and my lungs still grabbing at air that no longer resisted. . . . I sat down and looked about me and was suddenly very depressed." With success from *The Glass Menagerie* came suspicion. Williams found he no longer trusted even his friends. People seemed to be flattering him because of his fame, rather than giving him honest evaluations, and he began to doubt his skills as an artist. Partly in an attempt to escape from his new-found success, which seemed to be killing his spirit, Williams went into a hospital for an eye operation. For the past five years he had suffered with a cataract on his left eye, which required three needling operations. When the gauze mask was removed from his face in the hospital, he found himself in a readjusted world. "Well, the gauze mask served a purpose," he confessed. "While I was resting in the hospital the friends whom I had neglected or affronted in one way or another began to call on me and now that I was in pain and darkness, their voices seemed to have changed . . . once more they were sincere and kindly voices with the ring of truth in them and that quality of understanding for which I had originally sought them out.''

Believing that he could write more successfully if he were not surrounded by wealth and flattery, Williams decided to leave New York. He withdrew to Mexico and began to work on *The Poker Night,* which later was retitled *A Streetcar Named Desire.* In 1947, *Streetcar* opened on Broadway, receiving ecstatic reviews and enormous popular acclaim. Williams could no longer find anonymity anywhere. The success of *The Glass Menagerie* and *Streetcar* established him as one of the country's leading playwrights, and his life (as well as his works) became public property.

Later Plays

Williams has written and produced a play every two years since the opening of *The Glass Menagerie.* All the plays, except the most recent ones, have been financially successful; most of them have been well received critically. Among the most interesting are: *Summer and Smoke,* another play which, like *Streetcar,* depicts the conflict between the spirit and the flesh in the life of a southern gentlewoman; *The Rose Tattoo,* the story of Serafina della Rose's return to passion after the death of her husband; and *Camino Real,* a surrealistic play about a world of cruelty and decadence in which the man with ideals can barely survive. Other plays, like *Cat on a Hot Tin Roof, Sweet Bird of Youth, Period of Adjustment,* and *The Night of the Iguana,* have had less significant themes, but have been entertainingly written and commercially successful.

"Cathartic" Effect of Playwriting on Williams

In the summer of 1957, Williams decided to undergo psychoanalysis. With the commercial failures of his long plays, *Camino Real* and *Orpheus Descending,* he began to doubt himself as a writer. These doubts were accompanied by spells of claustrophobia and the fear that he might go blind altogether. (Williams *is* practically blind in his left eye.) While he was undergoing psychoanalytic treatment, he wrote a one-act play which he titled, *Suddenly Last Summer,* and which turned out to be one of Williams' greatest successes. This play was presented off-Broadway at the York Theatre with another one-act play, *Something Unspoken,* which had been written earlier. Williams has said that the writing of *Suddenly Last Summer* was for him a kind of ''catharsis.'' In a sense, this remark could be applied to all of Williams' plays, for they seem to be written out of a compulsive need to rid himself of his own fears and anxieties.

Chronology of Important Dates

1928   First story published in *Weird Tales.*

1929   Entered University of Missouri. Received small prizes for prose and poetry.

1931   Withdrawn by father for flunking ROTC and for financial reasons and put to work in International Shoe Co. warehouse. Spent long nights writing at home.

1935   After nervous breakdown, spent a year recuperating at home of grandparents in Memphis. First play, *Cairo! Shanghai! Bombay!* produced.

1936   Entered Washington University, St. Louis. *Candles in the Sun* and *Fugitive Kind* (not the later film script) produced.

1937   Entered University of Iowa, sister Rose underwent prefrontal lobotomy.

1938   Graduated from Iowa.

1939   Itinerant writer, wandering from Chicago to St. Louis, to New Orleans, to California, to New Mexico. Won Group Theater prize of $100 for *American Blues*. Awarded $1,000 Rockefeller Grant.

1940   Entered John Gassner's advanced playwriting seminar at New School, New York City. Failure of *Battle of Angels* in Boston.

1941-44 Lived and wrote in New Orleans and New York and worked as waiter-entertainer, elevator operator, and theater usher in New York, and as M-G-M script-writer in California.

1944   *The Glass Menagerie* opened in Chicago, December 26.

1945   *The Glass Menagerie* produced at the Playhouse, New York; directed by Eddie Dowling and Margo Jones. Won New York Critics' Circle Award. Published by Random House. Fourth unsuccessful operation for cataract on left eye.

1946   *27 Wagons Full of Cotton and Other Plays* published.

1947   *A Streetcar Named Desire* produced at the Barrymore Theatre, New York; directed by Elia Kazan. Won second New York Critics' Circle Award and Pulitzer Prize. Published by New Directions.

1948   *Summer and Smoke* produced at Music Box Theatre, New York; directed by Margo Jones. (Revived off-Broadway under José Quintero's direction in 1952.) *American Blues: Five Short Plays* published. *One Arm and Other Stories* published.

1950   Novel, *The Roman Spring of Mrs. Stone* published.

1951   *The Rose Tattoo* produced at Martin Beck Theatre, New York; directed by Daniel Mann. *I Rise in Flame, Cried the Phoenix* published.

1953   *Camino Real* produced at National Theatre, New York; directed by Elia Kazan (Revived under José Quintero's direction in 1960.)

1954   *Hard Candy: A Book of Stories* published.

1955   *Cat on a Hot Tin Roof* produced at Morosco Theatre, New York; directed by Elia Kazan. Won third New York Critics' Circle Award and second Pulitzer Prize.

1956   Film, *Baby Doll,* opened in New York. Poems, *In the Winter of Cities,* published.

1957   *Orpheus Descending* produced at Martin Beck Theatre, New York; directed by Harold Clurman. Began psychoanalysis.

1958   *Garden District (Something Unspoken* and *Suddenly Last Summer)* produced off-Broadway; directed by Herbert Machiz.

1959   *Sweet Bird of Youth* produced at Martin Beck Theatre, New York; directed by Elia Kazan.

1960   *Period of Adjustment* produced at Helen Hayes Theatre, New York; directed by George Roy Hill. Film, *The Fugitive Kind* (screen version of *Orpheus Descending*) opened in New York.

1961   *The Night of the Iguana* produced at Royale Theatre, New York; directed by Frank Corsaro. Won fourth New York Critics' Circle Award.

1962   First version of *The Milk Train Doesn't Stop Here Anymore* produced in Spoleto, Italy.

1963   Second version of *Milk Train* produced at Morosco Theatre, New York; directed by Herbert Machiz. Entered period of depression over death of intimate friend, Frank Merlo.

1964   First version of *The Eccentricities of a Nightingale* tried out in summer stock.

1966   *Slapstick Tragedy (The Mutilated* and *The Gnädiges Fräulein),* produced at Longacre Theatre, New York and directed by Alan Schneider, closed after seven performances.

1967   First version of *The Two-Character Play* produced at Hampstead Theatre Club, London. *The Knightly Quest: A Novella and Four Short Stories* published.

1968   *Kingdom of Earth (The Seven Descents of Myrtle)* produced at Ethel Barrymore Theatre, New York; directed by José Quintero.

1969   *In the Bar of a Tokyo Hotel,* produced off-Broadway and directed by Herbert Machiz, closed after twenty-five performances. Converted to Roman Catholicism. Admitted to St. Louis hospital after nervous collapse in Key West. Released three months later.

1970   *Dragon Country: A Book of Plays* published.

1971   First volume of *The Theatre of Tennessee Williams* published by New Directions.

Second version of *The Two-Character Play* (titled *Out Cry*) produced at Ivanhoe Theatre, Chicago.

1972   *Small Craft Warnings,* produced off-off-Broadway and directed by Richard Altman, was first commercial success since *Iguana.*

1973   Third version of *The Two-Character Play* (titled *Out Cry*), produced at Lyceum Theatre, New York, and directed by Peter Glenville, closed after twelve performances.

1974   *Eight Mortal Ladies Possessed: A Book of Stories* published.

1975   First version of *The Red Devil Battery Sign* closed in Boston and New York opening postponed. Second version of *Kingdom of Earth* produced in Princeton, N.J. Fourth version of *The Two-Character Play* produced off-off-Broadway. Novel, *Moise and the World of Reason* published. *Memoirs* published.

1976   Second version of *Red Devil* produced in Vienna; directed by Franz Schafranek. *This Is (An Entertainment)* produced in San Francisco; directed by Allen Fletcher. Fifth volume of *The Theatre of Tennessee Williams* published. Second version of *The Eccentricities of a Nightingale* produced in Buffalo, New York, and at Morosco Theatre, New York; directed by Edwin Sherin.

1977   *Vieux Carré* produced at St. James Theatre, New York; directed by Arthur Allan Seidelman.

Introduction to *The Glass Menagerie*

The Original Production

When Audrey Wood was first shown the script of *The Glass Menagerie,* which Williams had completed after he left his writing stint at M-G-M, she was impressed by the rare quality of the work and realized this play had to be submitted to a limited number of producers. Remembering that Eddie Dowling had introduced the plays of Paul Vincent Carroll to the United States, she decided to offer *The Glass Menagerie* first to this actor-producer-director. Dowling optioned the play at once and began the search for a financial backer. A banker, Louis J. Singer, put up $75,000, and the job of casting the play began.

Dowling had decided that he himself would direct the play. He was intrigued by the character of Tom, the poetic dreamer trapped by painful circumstances into a job in a warehouse, and although Dowling was middle-aged, he decided to play that role. For the part of Laura he chose the fragile, blonde actress, Julie Haydon, whom he had directed earlier in Sean O'Casey's *Shadow and Substance* and William Saroyan's *The Time of Your Life.* Anthony Ross was chosen to play the gentleman caller, Jim O'Connor.

Only the crucial part of Amanda remained to be cast. Dowling and the critic, George Jean Nathan, felt that no actress other than the legendary Laurette Taylor could play the part. Miss Taylor, following the death of her dramatist husband, Hartley Manners, had been on a downward spiral in her career. It was common gossip that she was an alcoholic. For this reason both Dowling and Williams were a little hesitant about approaching Miss Taylor with an offer, but the reluctance was far outweighed by their confidence in the actress' ability and "rightness" for the part of Amanda. They confronted her with a proposal and she accepted. Miss Taylor realized that through such a role she could regain her prominence in the theatrical world.

In December, 1944, after the usual weeks of rehearsal in New York City, the company left for a try-out run in Chicago.

Dowling, with the author's permission, decided to eliminate the elaborate screen devices Williams suggested in the original version of his play. The playwright, however, chose to retain the devices in the published version of the play. (See the section on the setting of *The Glass Menagerie* for a discussion of the screen devices.) Only a few other changes were made in Williams' play, although Miss Taylor, who had by now completely identified with the character of Amanda Wingfield, added some improvisation of her own making.

With magnificent setting and lighting designed by Jo Mielziner, *The Glass Menagerie* opened in Chicago's Civic Theatre on December 26, 1944. Led by the brilliant performance of Miss Taylor, the entire cast gave superlative portrayals.

The play and cast received excellent notices, but the audiences only half filled the theater. They continued to be disappointingly small, and the plans for bringing the play to New York were cancelled. It seemed as though the play would not run more than a limited number of weeks in Chicago. Sparked by a drive on the part of the Chicago drama critics, headed by Claudia Cassidy, and by enthusiastic word-of-mouth advertising, however, the crowds became larger. Soon they filled the theater, and tickets for this remarkable new play became extremely scarce. Dowling and the backers revived their intentions to open on Broadway.

On March 31, 1945, *The Glass Menagerie* opened at the Playhouse Theatre in New York City. The play was received with the same acclaim and enthusiasm that it finally had aroused in Chicago. Tennessee Williams was at once established as a leading new American playwright. Since then he has confirmed the dramatic ability exhibited by this delicate memory play. He has written more vigorous plays, but none more touching or fragile.

A few weeks after *The Glass Menagerie* opened, the play won the New York Drama Critics' Circle Award as the best play of the season. In addition, the play received the Donaldson Award, sponsored by *Billboard* magazine, and voted upon by people in show business. Laurette Taylor and Tony Ross received the *Billboard* acting awards. Williams was also awarded the Sidney Howard Memorial Award of $1,500 as the best new talent on Broadway.

The play ran for 565 performances and closed August 3, 1946. Laurette Taylor died soon after finishing her performance in this play. All of Broadway and Hollywood was saddened, and it was generally agreed that this last role had been her greatest.

Williams sold the motion picture rights to Charles K. Feldman who produced it — starring Gertrude Lawrence as Amanda Wingfield. This picture introduced a new actor to the screen, Kirk Douglas, as "The Gentleman Caller."

Theatrical and Literary Influences on the Play

As a dramatist, Tennessee Williams is more than a little indebted to the Russian playwright and short-story writer, Anton Chekhov. Chekhov's major influences are evidenced in Williams' careful development of mood and atmosphere. The Russian writer was a pioneer in the creation of psychologically motivated characters. Another striking feature of his work is the use of comedy in scenes of pathos. Williams carefully builds a mood of nostalgia in *The Glass Menagerie*. The characters in this play are well motivated, just as Chekhov's are. And *The Glass Menagerie,* although a touching and somewhat sentimental play, is filled with comedy. Both Williams and the Russian writer were concerned with the decline of aristocratic societies and the conflict between the old and the new social systems.

The Swedish dramatist, August Strindberg (1849-1912), has also influenced Williams. Strindberg, like Williams, had an unhappy childhood that he tried to interpret in terms of drama. A writer several decades before his time, Strindberg created strong characters plagued by internal conflicts. And like Williams, Strindberg did not hesitate to allow his characters to be destroyed by their own neuroses. It is from Strindberg that Williams gets the "memory play" technique. The sheer theatricality of Williams also links him to Strindberg. His minute attention to details of music and lighting is similar to that of the earlier dramatist. And they are similar in one other important respect: both writers were concerned with human suffering.

Williams has also been influenced by the father of modern drama, Henrik Ibsen. Ibsen is responsible for the conventional play form. Of course, in *The Glass Menagerie* Williams breaks somewhat from this form in that he adopts a new, unrealistic, poetic form that is indebted to the influence of Strindberg. And though Williams is more concerned with the interior world of his characters than is Ibsen, he uses Ibsen's technique of plot construction. *The Glass Menagerie* is not as realistic a play as are the plays of Ibsen, but it develops in the same logical, tightly constructed manner of Ibsen's plays. That Williams has broken away from the plot-conscious Norwegian is undeniable. But he has not abandoned the form of Ibsen; he has merely refined it and adapted it to a more subjective and psychological theater.

Williams matured into a theatrical world dominated by Thornton Wilder and Eugene O'Neill. In *Our Town,* produced in 1938, Wilder uses a narrator, the stage manager, who sets the scenes and explains the background and the action of the drama. In *The Skin of Our Teeth* (1942), Wilder has a character, Sabina, who stops occasionally to speak directly to the audience, commenting on the play as it progresses. Tom, in *The Glass Menagerie,* is a combination of these two characters. He is a stage manager, opening scenes, explaining the sociological background, introducing the characters, cueing the background music and the lighting. He is also a character in the play, and moves from the footlights into the set and back again.

Both *Our Town* and *The Skin of Our Teeth* are presented without realistic sets. *Our Town* uses a bare stage with barrels, boxes, and ladders to represent houses, a drugstore, and a cemetery. *The Skin of Our Teeth* has more elaborate sets, but the play is frequently produced with only the suggestions of walls and furniture. *The Glass Menagerie,* being a memory play, has need for only the simplest setting, suggestive rather than explicit.

Our Town is peopled with ordinary human beings; the Gibbses and the Webbs are the citizens of any town. *The Skin of Our Teeth* is concerned with Adam, Eve, Cain, and Lilith as they survive the Ice Age, the Flood, and World War I. Williams' characters in *The Glass Menagerie* are somewhere in between. They are not as fantastic as those in *The Skin of Our Teeth,* but they are somewhat removed from the reality of those in *Our Town.*

Although Williams does transcend the peculiar and the particular in *The Glass Menagerie,* he is less concerned with large universal questions than Wilder is in *Our Town* and *The Skin of Our Teeth.* The influence of Wilder's two plays on *The Glass Menagerie* is one of method, not of theme.

The shadow of Eugene O'Neill has dominated modern American drama. The affinity of Williams for O'Neill is revealed in their mutual concern and compassion for lost souls. O'Neill, however, is an epic dramatist whose concern is with universal frustration. Williams does not create broad, wide dramas (with the possible exceptions of *A Streetcar Named Desire* and *Orpheus Descending*), but instead concentrates on his individualized characters, indicating the universalities of love and suffering through the use of symbols. He is more of a poet in both the use of symbols and poetic mood and dialogue than is O'Neill. However, the influence of O'Neill is evident in both dramatic technique and choice of themes.

The British novelist, poet, and essayist, D. H. Lawrence, influenced Williams and his work very much. In all of his work, Lawrence complains bitterly that "civilization" has ruined man, causing him to surrender his individuality and become a part of a machine. Williams is much concerned with preserving the individuality and integrity of the human animal, a fact which is sharply delineated in Tom's hatred of the warehouse where he works, a place where he is expected to be an automaton.

Another of Lawrence's most pressing themes is that man has lost the ability to communicate with his fellows. Williams underlines that idea in *The Glass Menagerie*. Amanda, Laura, Tom, Mr. Wingfield— and to some degree Jim—cannot express to each other what they feel to be their essential natures, their ruling passions, and their goals. Amanda understands neither Tom nor Laura. Jim cannot understand Amanda, Laura, or Tom. Looking back from some distance and still haunted by the breakup of his family, Tom can, as narrator, understand Amanda and Laura. However, Tom as a character, and in the middle of the situation, cannot. Both Lawrence and Williams see modern society as working against the individual, keeping him from his rightful fulfillment.

A strong influence on *The Glass Menagerie* is the life and work of the American poet, Hart Crane. Williams has often remarked that he considers Crane's collection of poems, *The White Tower,* to be the most exciting lyrics that he has ever read. Crane frequently puts a great deal of strain on his symbols, making them do more work than symbols ordinarily are expected to do. One of the more valid adverse criticisms of *The Glass Menagerie* is that Williams frequently makes symbolism do the work that dialogue should do.

The most important influence of Crane on *The Glass Menagerie* is in Tom's idea of the proper life of the poet. Crane's father made him work in the family candy factory, a job the young poet detested. As soon as he could, Crane ran away, and he spent the rest of his short life almost constantly in transit, from New York to Florida to the Isle of Pines to Mexico to Europe. Tom, hating his mundane job in the shoe warehouse, thinks that to be a poet he must do the same. It is interesting to note that in his own life, Williams has been as restless as Crane, wandering from St. Louis to New Orleans to Los Angeles to Key West to New York and around the world several times.

Defining the Work: The Dream Play

Tennessee Williams matured as a writer while drama itself was in transition. For a hundred years, the picture-frame stage had dominated theater architecture, and realistic or naturalistic sets were thought of and treated as actual rooms with only one wall removed so that the audience could see in. With the WPA money of the 1930's, the American theater changed its face. Experimental theaters were created. Not dependent on box-office receipts for their existence, theater groups could explore the novel and the daring. Drama began to do what painting and music had done decades before—venture into abstraction, impressionism, and expressionism. Producers and directors realized that movies could handle realistic details much better than could the living stage. This latter form was realized to have a potential beyond that of displaying a "genuine frigidaire and authentic ice-cubes." Williams early association with the Mummers in St. Louis was fortunate. This lively group was daring in its experiments, frankly theatrical.

When Williams came to write *The Glass Menagerie,* he rejected the idea of casting it in a realistic mold. Since he wished to present it as a memory (it does have many autobiographical elements that make much of it a part of the playwright's own memory), he wrote suggestively, rather than literally. Certain elements of everyday life are omitted entirely, others are minimized, and still others are exaggerated. It is a series of events presented not as they actually took place, but as they might be remembered. Thus, the mistiness, the tenuousness, and the artificiality of it are justified by the point of view.

This is not to say that an unconventional play, such as this is, has the right to deviate from what another great southern writer, William Faulkner, called "the truth of the human heart." Williams accepts the responsibility of giving what he knows of the truth. Literalness is not necessarily truth; the poet in Williams recognizes this fact.

In *The Glass Menagerie* Williams is following in the path pioneered by the Swedish dramatist, August Strindberg. In 1906, Strindberg wrote in a preface to one of his own plays, "Time and space do not exist . . . But a single consciousness holds sway . . . that of the dreamer." In many respects that statement could be applied to Williams' play. *The Glass Menagerie* is episodic. It is dreamlike in its fragility. However, Tennessee Williams is not primarily an innovator. (See the section on theatrical and literary influences on *The Glass Menagerie.*) Much of the beauty of the play stems from this unconventional staging, but the greatness of the play stems from Williams' honest communication of human suffering.

The Setting

Until the time of George Bernard Shaw, few playwrights seemed to worry about how their plays were staged. We know the conventions of Shakespeare's stage, but that great playwright has left us no direct indication, in the form of prefaces, directions, descriptions of characters, etc., as to how he wished his work presented and interpreted. Many twentieth-century playwrights, however, have concerned themselves with the total audio-visual form that their works take on stage. Williams is such a playwright. He has inserted explicit directions, in the form of full stage directions and appended production notes, concerning the over-all sights and sounds of *The Glass Menagerie.*

Ideally, a play should be seen as well as read. This is not possible in many cases; most people must be content with only reading it. One does not read a play the way one reads a novel or a short story, however. He has to learn a new reading technique. He has to develop the ability to "see" what is going on as he reads the dialogue. This ability to "see" the play is particularly important in the case of *The Glass Menagerie*. The descriptions of the characters, the stage directions, and the production notes are too important to be skipped over. In fact, much of the power of the play is lost (as well as much of its beauty) if the reader is inattentive to these details.

Although the original production of *The Glass Menagerie* has been adapted successfully to both projecting platform and arena staging, Williams has prefaced the play with explicit details of a set intended for a conventional proscenium, or picture-frame, stage. When the curtain rises, the audience is confronted with a bare exterior wall of a brick tenement building. Williams describes these tenements as "hive-like conglomerations of cellular living-units," thereby indicating that they are more fit for insects than for human beings. This is another indication of what he considers to be the depersonalization of man in a machine-oriented society. Bees are very efficient and well-organized laborers, but they are not individuals. There are alleys running down both sides of this particular cell, off into the wings, cluttered with garbage cans, clothes lines, and the usual trash that accumulates in the back alleys of lower-middle-class apartment buildings. The only other exterior feature is a fire escape, which serves as the entrance to the Wingfield apartment. It is, Williams says, exactly what its name states, the only "escape" that the Wingfields have from their rather dingy set of rooms. It is the only place to go to cool off on warm evenings, and it is in ironic contrast to the cool high galleries and balconies that Amanda knew as a girl in Blue Mountain. When Tom is acting as narrator, he stands either downstage at the footlights or on this fire escape.

During his first speech, the light comes on behind the tenement wall, turning it into a transparent screen. During the opening speeches of the first scene, the wall is slowly raised, and the interior of the Wingfield's front room becomes a kind of stage within a stage. The tenement wall is lowered again only during Tom's final speech. The dining room, which is far upstage, is framed by an arch, becoming another inner stage. Thus, the effect is much like that of Chinese boxes or an exercise in perspective drawing, leading the eye to the point far upstage where all the lines seem to converge. The dining room arch is closed by portieres which are at times made transparent by the lights behind them, at times left opaque, at times pulled back and tied.

As Williams has pointed out, this is a "memory play," and it is not at all necessary to have a realistic or naturalistic set. There are few important pieces of furniture in the front room: a sofa which pulls down into a bed for Laura, a table and chair, and an old-fashioned stand on which Laura's glass menagerie is displayed. In the last scene, a new floor lamp with a rose-colored shade is added. The only other features of the room are a large framed photograph of Mr. Wingfield which hangs to the (audience's) left of the dining room arch, and charts of a typewriter keyboard and Gregg shorthand symbols, which are on the wall over the living room table during the first two scenes. The only furniture visible in the dining room is a dining table and chairs. There are windows in the front room which open onto the alleys, and a door in the dining room which leads to the kitchen.

During the first five scenes of the play, the two rooms are very drab, both the walls and the furniture showing much decay. For the last two scenes, there is Amanda's pitiful attempt to spruce things up. In addition to the new floor lamp, there are bright, summery chintz covers on the sofa and chair, and billowing, fresh curtains at the windows. These touches serve only to point up the basic drabness of the rooms, however.

The Lighting

Although a discussion of the lighting of a play is ordinarily extraneous to a consideration of its literary worth, the fact that Williams concerned himself with the details of production and saw the play as an integrated whole, made up of both auditory and visual effects, makes such a discussion pertinent here. Produced or read with a disregard to what the playwright wants the audience to see, *The Glass Menagerie* would lose much of its great power.

Just as the set itself is sparse and formalized, so should the lighting be theatrical rather than realistic. Williams has indicated in his production notes that when she is on the stage—even when she is not participating actively in the conversations of the characters—Laura should be given special attention by the use of lighting, and wherever she is should be the visual center of the stage. The light on her should be a pure white, not harsh but clear. The playwright has likened the kind of light he wishes to that in religious pictures during the Renaissance, in which faces are luminous and backgrounds are somewhat obscured in shadow.

Another important use of symbolic lighting is in Scene 3. During Tom's quarrel with Amanda, the stage is lit in a smoky red glow. The redness is appropriate both to the anger that mother and son exhibit and to the historical event which is always present in the background of the play, the war in Spain (1936-39). Europe is about to go up in flames. As Tom reads the war news, he feels the need for adventure more deeply and urgently. While he is a clerk in a shoe warehouse, part of the world is burning.

The lighting on Amanda is frequently harsh. In Scene 4, it gives her the appearance of a Daumier print. Daumier, a nineteenth-century French artist, was noted for his naturalistic treatment of everyday urban life through a method that showed his training as a political cartoonist. The faces of his peasants, soldiers, and bureaucrats are often quite ugly and nearly always harshly lit. Ironically, while Amanda is shown in this same kind of light, the background music is "Ave Maria."

In Scene 5, there is a suggestion of gaudy lights coming from the Paradise Dance Hall across the alley, and occasional colored beams from the prismatic mirrored globe that Tom describes. Its vain attempt to provide beauty and wonder only points up the discrepancy between desire and realization.

The lighting in Scene 7 also deserves special attention. When Amanda displays herself, dressed in the yellow frock from her Blue Mountain days, harsh lighting on her underlines the cruelty of the caricature. In the long scene between Jim and Laura, the only obvious source of light on the stage is from the candelabrum. There is, of course, light from other sources, since a few candles could not provide enough illumination for the audience to see the actors, but it is made to "seem" that the obvious source is the only one. There is the clear beam of white light always on Laura, and there is enough lighting from below to throw Jim's shadow distinctly onto the upper walls and the ceiling.

The Music

A young American author and composer named Paul Bowles was commissioned to write the music for the original production of *The Glass Menagerie*. Bowles, a wanderer who moved to North Africa, is probably best known for his novel, *The Sheltering Sky,* and his collection of short stories, *The Delicate Prey.* In their fiction—and in their private lives—Williams and Bowles are kindred spirits, and it is fitting that Bowles should have scored Williams' play.

The dominant theme is, of course, "The Glass Menagerie," a wispy, never-never melody played on the violin. It acts as a kind of leitmotif, or recurring theme, associated with Laura and her glass animals. When Laura retreats into her world of delicate little animals, this music is always in the background.

There is other music in the play, most of it the blaring honkytonk music of the 1930's, originating across the alley in the Paradise Dance Hall. It is hot, sexually oriented music which contrasts well with the cool purity of the "Glass Menagerie" theme. It is from a world that neither Amanda nor Laura knows, a world that Tom occasionally visits in abortive attempts at adventure. It is the false front of gaiety that the Depression pulls over its real face of desperation.

The Screen Device

Present in the published play, but not used in its original production, are instructions for the projection of legends and pictures on the back wall of the Wingfield's living room. They were intended to be shown, by rear screen projection, probably on the wall to the (audience's) right of the archway leading to the dining room. Williams intended these phrases and photographs to point up important elements of motivations, characterization, and theme. With such a function, they are of some help in studying the play.

SCENE 1

The legend at the opening of the scene is "ou sont les neiges?"—"Where are the snows (of yesteryear)?"—the refrain of a poem by the medieval French poet, Francois Villon. This is probably the most famous poem in Western literature to depict the sadness and melancholy of man over the good things that he once had, and now has lost. Tom is looking back from the 1940's to the late 1930's—to a period before the complete dissolution of his family. Amanda, from the 1930's, looks back to her girlhood in Blue Mountain, Mississippi. Both see their yesterdays as better times than they are now experiencing. The legend from a medieval poem lends a kind of universality to their particular melancholy. Signi Falk, in her, *Tennessee Williams,* claims that Villon's tribute to the beautiful women in his past life is singularly inappropriate to represent Amanda's melancholy over her lost Blue Mountain girlhood, a point which is worth considering.

SCENE 2

During Laura's painful account of her horror of going back to business college, there is the image of a swarm of typewriters on the screen, representative not only of Laura's fears but of the mechanization and impersonality of modern life. The image of the park in winter, also in this scene, seems superfluous; and the legend "The Crust of Humility" that is on the screen while Amanda is indulging in self-pity seems to be an attempt at irony, which seems inappropriate to the characterization of the mother here. The image of blue roses, which is shown while Laura speaks of her high school relationship to Jim, also presents a problem. A part of the appropriateness of the nickname, "Blue Roses," is the fact that such flowers don't exist, and it is rather hard to believe that they don't exist while looking at a picture of them.

SCENE 3

This scene opens with the legend "After the fiasco—," which are also the first three words of Tom's first speech. Rather quickly, this legend gives way to the image of a young man with flowers at the door, the "gentleman caller," which is becoming Amanda's obsession. Ironically—perhaps too much so—while Amanda is discussing *The Homemaker's Companion,* a magazine supposedly for middle-class and middle-aged women, the image on the screen is the cover of a glamor magazine. During the quarrel between Amanda and Tom over the D. H. Lawrence book that Amanda took back to the library, the legend is "You think I'm in love with Continental Shoemakers?"—rather too obvious to be effective. At the end of the scene, when Tom throws his coat and accidentally knocks some of Laura's little animals from the stand, the legend is "The Glass Menagerie." Since the focus of the action is already on the symbolic little pieces of glass, the legend seems superfluous.

SCENE 4

The legend "Laura" appears on the screen while Tom and Amanda are discussing her. When Tom talks about his need for adventure, there is the image of a pirate ship flying a Jolly Roger, which makes his craving seem a little ridiculous. Again, as Amanda calls a subscriber of *The Homemaker's Companion,* there is the image of a glamor magazine.

SCENE 5

This scene opens with the legend "Annunciation," another of Williams' imperfectly realized religious symbols. He seems to equate the announcement to the Virgin Mary that she is to bear the Christ to Tom's announcement to his mother that Laura will have a gentleman caller. When Tom does tell his mother, the legend fades into the image of the gentleman caller with a bouquet of flowers.

SCENE 6

As Tom describes Jim O'Connor, the image on the screen is that of a high school hero, which changes to that of a clerk as Tom tells of Jim's less than meteoric rise in the world since leaving high school. As Amanda prepares Laura for Jim's visit, the legend is "The accent of a coming foot," which smacks of melodrama. After Amanda places the "gay deceivers" in Laura's bosom, the legend is "A pretty trap," which quickly changes to "This is my sister: celebrate her with strings!"—intended no doubt to be sincere, but again melodramatic in spite of itself. Three legends follow in rather quick succession: "Not Jim!"—"Terror!"—"The opening of a door!" All of them seem overly obvious and, again, melodramatic. In their little talk before supper, Tom and Jim are contrasted in the images flashed on the screen for each: for Jim, the picture of an executive at a desk; for Tom, the pirate ship again. When Amanda comes out dressed in her ancient frock and shaking her girlish ringlets, there is the image of her as a girl. When Laura is forced to come to the table, the legend reads "Terror!" again, and when she nearly faints, it changes to "Ah!"—which is probably the least effective, and the most unintentionally humorous, of all the legends.

SCENE 7

This last scene opens with the legend "A Souvenir," pointing forward to Laura's giving Jim the little unicorn, and pathetically suggesting that this evening will be nothing more than a souvenir, something to remember and not the beginning of a new relationship. When the lights go out, there is the coldly impersonal legend "Suspension of a public service," aptly suggestive of corporate indifference to the plight of little people. When Amanda realizes that Tom did not pay the light bill, the legend changes to "Ha!"—another rather facetious remark. After the meal, as Jim and Laura begin to talk to each other, the legend is "I don't suppose you remember me at all!"—which is appropriate, since Jim does not remember Laura without some hints from her. After they discuss their days at Soldan High School, the legend changes to "What have you done since high school?" This is appropriate for both, since Laura has drifted pretty much without purpose in the last six years and Jim has not made the mark in the world that he thinks he should have made by now. After their waltz, Jim tells Laura how pretty she is, and the image on the screen is "Blue Roses." He kisses her, and the legend "Souvenir" appears. The next legend on the screen—"Love!"—is ironically meant for another girl, not Laura, as Jim tells of his fiancée. As Jim tells Laura that he will not call on her again, the legend reads "Things have a way of turning out so badly!" —an expression that appears a little trite at this highly moving spot. Williams has suggested an alternate to this legend, the image of a gentleman caller waving goodbye—gaily. Both seem intrusive. When Amanda hears from Jim that he is engaged, the legend reads "The sky falls." As Tom leaves at the end of the scene, the last legend appears: "And so good-bye. . . ."

Williams writes in the production notes to the play that the legends and images were designed to reinforce the most important point (or points) in each scene, to give thematic unity to an otherwise too episodic play. The fact is, as the power of the produced play attests, that the drama has sufficient unity and that the major points are clear enough without these artificial devices. In all probability, if they were used in a production, they would call too much attention to themselves, detracting from the playwright's powerful and effective dialogue.

Nevertheless, Williams seems fond of the device. He suggests that it has a much greater range of usage than he can possibly exploit in *The Glass Menagerie*. Perhaps it has an emotional appeal for him because it suggests the captions of the silent films that he saw in his youth.

Characters in the Play

TOM WINGFIELD: Tom is the narrator of the play and a character in it. He supports the family by his job in a shoe warehouse. He is a poet and feels that his responsibilities and unexciting life are crushing his individuality and his creative ability.

AMANDA WINGFIELD: Amanda is Tom's mother. She has held her family together since her husband deserted them years ago.

Part of her life is led in the genteel past of her youth. But she can never totally escape the real world of poverty and brutality.

LAURA WINGFIELD: Laura is Tom's sister. She is fragile and slightly crippled. She is unable to cope with reality and so lives in her own world of delicately sculpted glass animals and old phonograph records.

JIM O'CONNOR: Jim is an ordinary young man who worked with Tom at the shoe warehouse. In high school he was very popular and voted the boy "most likely to succeed," but since then he has not achieved all that he thinks he should have accomplished. He is the gentleman caller that Amanda and Laura have waited for so long to arrive.

MR. WINGFIELD: Mr. Wingfield is Tom's father, who deserted his family. He symbolizes escape and adventure for Tom. To Amanda he is the "telephone man who fell in love with long distances." He is present in the play only in the form of a photograph over the mantel in the Wingfield's living room.

Plot Summary

The Wingfield family, consisting of Tom, Amanda and Laura Wingfield, lives in a shabby apartment in St. Louis. Tom works at a warehouse and writes poetry in the times that he is not working or at the movies. Amanda sells magazine subscriptions from her home to supplement the family income. Laura has been enrolled in a business college. At dinner, Amanda lectures Tom on his table manners and tells Laura she must stay fresh and pretty for her gentlemen callers. Although Laura tells her mother that she is not expecting any gentlemen callers, Amanda recalls that when she was a young girl back in Blue Mountain she had so many gentlemen callers that one day they had to send for folding chairs from the church next door. Amanda then tells Laura that she must practise her typing and shorthand.

A few days later, Amanda comes home shocked. She has been to Laura's business college and found out that Laura dropped out of school several months ago. She wonders what will happen to her daughter since Laura spends all her time playing with her glass animals and listening to her old, worn-out phonograph records. Amanda asks Laura if she ever liked a boy. Laura replies that she once liked a boy in high school named Jim.

During an argument in which Amanda accuses Tom of drinking and doing something other than going to the movies, Tom calls Amanda a witch. She refuses to speak to him until he apologizes. After Laura pleads with him, Tom apologizes to his mother. Amanda asks him to find some nice unmarried young man and bring him home for dinner. She has decided that since Laura cannot have a business career, she must have a husband. A few days later, Tom tells Amanda that he has invited a young man he works with home for dinner. Amanda begins to make "plans and provisions" for entertaining the expected gentleman caller.

The next night, Amanda dresses Laura and gives her some "gay deceivers" to correct her flat chest. Laura is more beautiful than she has ever been, but when she hears the name of the gentleman caller she becomes very nervous. She knows it is the same young man she liked in high school. She refuses to answer the door when Tom and the young man arrive, but Amanda forces her to the door. At dinner, Laura must be excused; she is physically sick.

Later, Laura loses some of her timidity as Jim talks to her warmly. Jim is very attracted by the tender beauty of Laura, but after kissing her and seeing how serious both of them are becoming, he must explain that he is already engaged. When Amanda finds out that Jim is engaged, she thinks that Tom knew about it and was playing a cruel trick on them. Laura has sunk deeper and deeper into her world of glass figurines and Amanda comforts her. The play ends with Tom several years in the future. He has been fired from his job and joined the Merchant Marine. In the final speech he admits that he has never been able to forget his sister.

Scene Summaries and Commentaries

Instead of acts, the play is divided into parts. Part I, consisting of the first five scenes, is labeled "Preparation for a Gentleman Caller"; Part II, made up of Scenes 6 and 7, is called "The Gentleman Caller."

PART I · SCENE 1

Summary

The play opens on an alley that runs behind a tenement building in a poor and overcrowded section of St. Louis. Tom Wingfield, the narrator and one of the play's four major characters, enters the alley dressed as a merchant marine. After crossing to a fire escape, which also serves as the entrance to the Wingfield apartment, he addresses the audience. He describes the social background of the play: the depression years of the thirties, when America was about to enter World War II. He mentions the three other characters: his mother, Amanda; his sister, Laura; and a "gentleman caller," named Jim O'Connor. Referring to the latter, he explains that Jim is a symbol of "the long delayed but always expected something that we live for." A fifth character, Tom's father, does not appear in the play, but his portrait hanging in the Wingfield's living room is a constant reminder of his absence. He was a telephone man who, unable to face the responsibility of taking care of his family, gave up his job and disappeared from town. The last they heard of him was a picture postcard from Mexico which bore the brief message, "Hello—Good-bye!" As Tom finishes introducing the characters, the interior of the Wingfield apartment lights up. Amanda is seen sitting with Laura at a dropleaf table. They are about to have dinner and are awaiting Tom.

Tom leaves the stage to reappear a moment later in his place at the table. From this point on he functions as both narrator and as a character in the play. At dinner, Amanda, a middle-aged, southern belle who seems bent on directing the lives of her children, admonishes Tom on how to eat and digest his food. Exasperated by her incessant chatter, Tom leaves the table in a fit of anger. This incident serves to establish the tense atmosphere in the house. As the scene continues, the tension increases when Amanda reminds Laura she must stay fresh and pretty for gentlemen callers. Laura, who is crippled (one leg is slightly shorter than the other and held in a brace), says she is not expecting any gentlemen callers. Amanda replies airily that sometimes they appear when least expected. To prove her point, she relates a story that both Tom and Laura have heard many times before. When Amanda was a young, carefree girl in Blue Mountain, Mississippi, seventeen gentlemen callers visited her in one afternoon. As the story unfolds, her face lights up and her voice becomes rhapsodic. Caught in the illusion of the past, she explains that most of the callers who vied for her affections were "prominent young planters." And she emphasizes that she was a brilliant conversationalist who knew how to entertain her guests. When Tom asks her what she talked about, she says, "Things of importance going on in the world! Never anything coarse or common or vulgar." The romantic life Amanda describes is in direct contrast to the dismal reality of the present life she is living. She ends her tale by again reminding Laura that she, too, will have gentlemen callers. Laura shyly remarks that she is not a popular girl like Amanda was in Blue Mountain. Tom utters a groan of despair, and the scene dims as Laura confesses that she will probably be an old maid.

Commentary

The fire escape is used symbolically to represent various aspects of being trapped and as a method of escape. As Williams writes, the "huge buildings are always burning with the slow and implacable fires of human desperation." The play then presents Tom's frustrated attempt to escape from his intolerable job, situation, and life. For Amanda, the escape is seen in terms of the gentleman caller who will rescue her daughter from potential old-maidhood. But then, for Laura the escape is seen as her means of retreating (or escaping) from the outer world. It is her protection from this outside world—a world which stares at her deformity. In other words, whereas for Tom, it is an escape *to* the outer world, for Laura it is an escape *from* an outer world which she dreads so much. This will be symbolically portrayed later in the play when Amanda forces Laura to go to the store and Laura trips on the fire escape, symbolizing her dread of the hostile outside world.

Use of the narrator: The technique of using a narrator is often considered a trick by the artist so that he will not have to conceive of imaginative ways to convey exposition—that is, ways of communicating background information necessary to the present understanding of the play. (For example, a traditional technique, used by Henrik Ibsen, was to have two servants—one newly hired and one regular—on stage talking about their master and in this way, the audience learned all that was necessary in order to understand the present action.)

The use of Tom, however, is integrated into the play. He presents the play as a memory and then steps back into time to become one of the participants in the action.

In his opening monologue, Tom says that the stage magician "gives you illusion that has the appearance of truth. I give you truth in the pleasant disguise of illusion." Here, he means that the regular dramatist creates a dramatic illusion on the stage which the audience takes for the truth. But this play, by its techniques, offers itself as illusion; Williams maintains that it is actually truth disguised as illusion.

Even though this is a short scene, note that the author has carefully filled it with most of the essential meanings of the entire play. The nagging, the gentleman caller, Tom's restlessness, and Laura's shyness are all presented in this first scene. The fact that Amanda tells Laura to practise her shorthand and to study the typing chart prepares the reader for the beginning of the next scene where Amanda discovers Laura's deception about her failure in school.

SCENE 2

Summary

It is several days later. Laura is seated in the living room polishing her collection of glass animals. Amanda appears on the fire escape steps. At the sound of her footsteps, Laura quickly puts the glass menagerie away and sits stiffly at attention before a typewriter, as though she were concentrating on a lesson. Amanda enters the room, her face set grimly. She goes over to the wall near Laura and removes a typing chart which she tears to pieces. She does the same thing with a Gregg alphabet chart. She then sinks wearily onto a sofa and stares hopelessly at Laura. A moment later, she reveals the cause of her distress. That morning she discovered that Laura, who is enrolled in a secretarial course at Rubicam's Business College, has not been attending classes. This discovery shocked Amanda so deeply that she did not go to a planned DAR meeting, but returned home immediately. Amanda's high hopes for her daughter's future in the business world have been dashed. She is inconsolable, and accuses Laura of "deception."

Laura explains nervously that she became sick and almost fainted when the teacher at the school gave her a typing speed test. "I couldn't face it," she confesses. Amanda becomes suspicious. She wants to know what Laura has been doing with her time. Laura tells her that she has just been walking. Amanda does not believe her and presses her for details. Laura explains that she has spent her days wandering through the city, visiting museums, the zoo, and sometimes attending movies.

Amanda is appalled by Laura's apparent disinterest in her future. She assumes a martyred look and asks her if she intends to spend the rest of her life amusing herself with her glass menagerie, and playing old phonograph records which her father left behind when he deserted them. She goes on to describe the life of dependency and loneliness that awaits spinsters who have no source of income. "Little birdlike women without any nest—eating the crust of humility all their life!" she explodes. She then asks Laura if she has ever cared for a boy. Laura remembers a boy in high school named Jim. He sang in the senior class operetta and was very popular among his schoolmates. She shows Amanda a yearbook that contains Jim's picture. She recalls that he used to call her "Blue Roses" because she once had an attack of pleurosis. She adds that he must have married the girl he used to date, since their engagement was announced in the paper six years ago.

As Laura talks about Jim, Amanda's disappointment gives way to a rising mood of hope. Her vitality suddenly begins to reassert itself. She decides that the solution to Laura's problem is marriage. She tells Laura that girls who are unsuited for business careers usually wind up married to some "nice young man." Laura reminds her mother that she is crippled. Amanda forbids her to use that word, and assures her that she is only suffering from a slight defect, "hardly noticeable." Amanda refuses to acknowledge Laura's shy and introverted nature. She insists that all Laura has to do is cultivate charm. Charm will compensate for her defect, and bring her a husband and happiness. Amanda looks at the grinning photograph of Laura's father on the wall. Charm, she says ruefully, was the one thing he had plenty of.

Commentary

In the first episode, Amanda had told Laura to go practise her shorthand. At the opening of this scene, we see that Laura rapidly hides her glass ornaments and acts as though she is practising her typing when she hears Amanda ascending the fire escape. This scene, then, reveals that Laura has not been going to her school.

This revelation has a devastating effect on Amanda. First, it represents a fifty dollar loss of the tuition money—money which was very hard to come by. But more important, it forces Amanda to consider the future and to face realistically problems that she does not like to think about—that is, that she has a daughter who is crippled and who is too sensitive to work. These thoughts, in turn, bring to Amanda's mind the need for a gentleman caller.

Note how Amanda plays the revelation scene for all its theatrical effect. This is also a part of her character and prepares us for her giddy actions when the gentleman caller comes.

SCENE 3

Summary

Tom addresses the audience again as narrator. He describes the developments in the house since the fiasco at Rubicam's Business College. Several months have gone by and it is now early spring. The idea of getting a husband for Laura has become an obsession in Amanda's mind. In order to gain a little extra income to fix up the apartment and make Laura more attractive for a gentleman caller, she has taken to soliciting magazine subscriptions. The light dims on Tom and a spotlight reveals Amanda at the telephone trying vainly to sell a subscription to a housewife.

A moment later, Tom enters the room and becomes involved in an argument with his mother. He accuses her of confiscating his books. She admits she took one of his books back to the library, a novel by D. H. Lawrence, which she thought highly immoral. When Tom laughs at her narrow-minded objections, she screams, "I won't allow such filth brought into my house!" Angrily, Tom starts to leave the apartment, but Amanda orders him back.

Tom is a young poet with a job in a shoe factory, a job that is slowly crushing his spirit, but which he keeps to support his family. He dreams of becoming a great writer, but is trapped by his job and the insupportable emotional situation at home with Amanda. His only escape is the movies, where he goes night after night to lose himself in the manufactured fantasies of Hollywood. Amanda does not believe that he goes to the movies: she is convinced that he is doing things which he should be ashamed of. Tom finally becomes infuriated at his mother's absurd accusations. His frustration breaks out and he shouts at his mother, making it clear that he hates his job, hates the life he is leading, and would rather die than go back to the Continental Shoemakers! He then starts to leave the house again, informing his mother that he is going to the movies. Amanda, shaken by her son's wrath, tries to stop him, and Tom calls her an ugly, babbling, old witch.

Seizing his overcoat, he lunges to the door, but because of his anger his arm catches in the sleeve, and he rips the coat off, hurling it across the room. It falls on the shelf where Laura keeps her collection of glass, and breaks several of the tiny glass animals. Laura, who has been standing throughout this scene listening nervously to the quarrel between her brother and mother, gasps as the glass shatters. The glass menagerie represents escape from reality to Laura—a shimmering, fragile world wherein she can hide. Now she cries out in pain, as though part of her secret self had been wounded. But Amanda is too shocked by Tom's insult to notice Laura's consternation. She rallies her composure and informs Tom that she will never speak to him again until he apologizes for calling her a witch. She then leaves the room.

Tom is left alone with Laura, who has turned weakly to the mantel. Realizing that he has hurt his sister by his rash act, and feeling guilty, he falls on his knees and tries to pick up the shattered glass figurines. He glances at Laura and tries to speak to her, but he cannot.

Commentary

One of Amanda's admirable qualities is her determination. Once she has set her mind to a task, she goes about it with a determination that neither of her children possesses. It would be impossible to imagine either Tom or Laura dedicating themselves to a task with such complete zeal as does Amanda.

It is, however, this dedication which makes her appear hateful to her children. It is as though both, especially Tom, were still youths whose every action has to be supervised.

It is interesting to note that Williams has Tom reading a novel by D. H. Lawrence. Lawrence was a British novelist, essayist, and poet of the early twentieth century. He advocated taking love out of the head (where it has been intellectualized into frigidity and impotence) and putting it back into the body where he felt that it belonged. A happy relationship between two people is possible only where there is a free and complete sexual union between them. A victim of tuberculosis, Lawrence spent several of his last years in New Mexico, with his wife Frieda. Williams visited her there after her husband's death.

In the 1930's and 1940's, Williams was much interested in Lawrence's life and work. With Donald Windham, he wrote a play based on Lawrence's story *You Touched Me!* (produced in 1945, the year after *The Glass Menagerie*). In 1951, Williams published a one-act play based on the life of Lawrence, *I Rise in Flame, Cried the Phoenix,* performed at two ANTA matinees.

Amanda's over-protectiveness has caused Tom to lash out blindly, hurting—unintentionally—both her and his sister. If he hates his mother at this moment, that hate is only momentary. He will be sorry for it later.

He realizes immediately that he has hurt Laura by his thoughtless act, but is powerless to communicate an apology to her. This inability to communicate is one of the major themes of the play. All three major characters live in different worlds—none of them quite the real world—and none can explain his world to either of the others.

SCENE 4

Summary

It is five in the morning. A nearby church bell is booming out the hour. Tom appears, slightly intoxicated, on the fire escape steps. Laura hears him and opens the door. He tells her that he has just come from an all-night movie which also featured a remarkable stage show. The headliner on this show was Malvolio the Magician who, besides performing such wonderful tricks as turning water into whiskey, managed to get out of a sealed coffin without removing a nail. "That is a trick that would come in handy for me—get me out of this 2-by-4 situation!" Tom says, as Laura helps him to bed. He then wonders hopelessly how anyone could ever get out of a coffin without removing a nail. As if in answer, the portrait of Tom's father lights up. The scene dims out and immediately comes up again.

An hour has passed. Amanda's voice is heard calling "Rise and Shine!" Tom sits up sleepily. "I'll rise," he says, "but I won't shine!" Even though his mother has called him, she is still determined not to talk with him until he apologizes for his remark of the preceding night. Amanda sends Laura to the grocery store, and she and Tom are left confronting each other in awkward silence. Finally, Tom, clutching his morning cup of coffee, blurts out an apology to Amanda. His mother draws a quick breath of relief and breaks into tears. She tells Tom that she has had to put up a solitary battle for years to keep her family together, and that he must not fail her. Her whole life revolves around her desire for her children's happiness. But she is afraid of one thing, that Tom will turn out to be a drunkard as his father was.

Tom grins sheepishly and dutifully promises Amanda that he will never be a drunkard. Amanda then confesses that she sent Laura to the grocery store so that she could discuss something of great importance with Tom. She goes on to say that she knows Tom's ambitions do not lie in the shoe factory, but, like everybody else in this difficult world, he has had to make "sacrifices." She says there are things in her heart which she cannot describe, things she's never told Tom. "I—*loved* your father," she admits emotionally. Tom tells her that there are things in his heart, too, which he finds difficult to talk to her about. In spite of the lack of communication between mother and son, it is obvious that they are deeply attached to each other.

Finally, Amanda says that she must talk about Laura. Tom listens patiently as she explains that she is frightened at the prospect of Laura just drifting along doing nothing. "We have to be making some plans and provisions for her," she insists. She then reveals that she has seen a letter from the Merchant Marine, and is aware that Tom plans to leave them. She adds it is all right for him to go, providing he will find somebody to take his place. When Tom asks her what she means, she answers that Laura must get married and have a home of her own.

Amanda is aware of the fact that Laura is drifting farther and farther away from reality into a world of her own making, symbolized by the collection of glass animals. As Tom starts to leave for work, Amanda pleads with him to help his sister. There must be some nice "clean-living" young man down at the shoe factory who doesn't drink and would be suitable for Laura. She begs Tom to find such an eligible paragon of virtue. Tom, to get away from his mother, says "yes," he will try to find a gentleman caller for his sister. He leaves and, a moment later, Amanda, now brimming with hope, hurries to the telephone to call up another potential magazine subscriber.

Commentary

When Tom returns from the movies, he emphasizes his desire to escape by talking about the magician who was nailed in a coffin and got out. He then compares his apartment and his situation in life to that of the magician climbing into a coffin—now the question is how he can get out of *his* coffin.

Notice that Laura trips on the outside fire escape, a device used to suggest her fear of the outside world.

As soon as Tom apologizes to his mother, she maintains (theatrically) that her devotion has made her a witch and hateful to her children. There is a great deal of truth in this statement. Her over-zealous devotion causes her to nag and almost persecute them.

The difference between Amanda and Tom is most clearly seen in this scene in their discussion of *instinct*. Tom is the poet and feels that man should live by his feelings and by his instinct. He feels that he is being destroyed as an individual by being forced to live all cramped up in the apartment and in the city. He seeks love, adventure, and romance. But these are the very qualities that Amanda's husband possessed; he followed his instincts and left home. Thus, Amanda views instinct as something bestial and vulgar. She wants a comfortable life within the bounds of prescribed propriety. Furthermore, Amanda is unable to recognize that her children have views different from hers.

SCENE 5

Summary

It is evening. The Wingfields have just finished supper, and Tom is slouching on the sofa reading a newspaper. He rises and steps out onto the fire escape from which he once again addresses the audience as narrator. He describes the Paradise Dance Hall, directly across from the alley, where people go to escape from the tedium of their existences. He talks about the approach of World War II, and how most people, including the Wingfields, have withdrawn into illusions of various kinds to avoid facing reality.

At the conclusion of Tom's speech, Amanda comes out of the

apartment and sits down on the landing steps beside him. There is a moon rising in the sky and Amanda makes a wish on it. She tells Tom that she wishes for "success and happiness for my precious children!" Tom counters by saying that he thought perhaps she wished for a gentleman caller. Amanda curiously asks him why he said that, and when Tom tells her that he has invited one of his fellow workers home from the shoe factory, she is elated. The young man is coming the following evening, and Amanda is worried because she feels she does not have enough time to prepare for his arrival. Windows have to be washed, fresh curtains put up, and a number of other important things attended to. Tom tells her that she is making too much of a fuss, but Amanda insists that she must work like a "Turk" to make the place presentable. She orders Tom into the apartment to question him about the young man.

"What is his name?" she asks. "His name is O'Connor," Tom replies. And after more pressing questions, Tom assures his mother that O'Connor is a suitable gentleman caller for Laura; he does not drink and he is ambitious to get ahead. As Amanda talks on about the imminent gentleman caller, Tom reminds her that he is just coming for supper and that lots of young men are introduced to girls whom they don't marry. But Amanda hardly hears him. Her mind is buzzing with plans. She is sure that once O'Connor sees how pretty and sweet Laura is, he will "thank his lucky stars he was asked to dinner." Tom tells her that she mustn't expect too much from Laura. He points out that she is terribly shy and lives in a world of her own, which makes some people think she is odd. Tom leaves for the movies and Amanda, convinced that this is Laura's great opportunity, calls her from the kitchen. When Laura appears, her mother takes her by the hand and tells her to make a wish on the moon. Bewildered by Amanda's impulsive order, Laura looks up at the moon and asks her what she should wish for. Amanda says hopefully, "Happiness! Good fortune!"

Commentary

This is an important part of the social significance of the play. During the Spanish Civil War, Franco, a fascist, sought to establish a reactionary, totalitarian government. In his attempt, he was aided by the rich landowners and—significantly—by Hitler's Germany. Most of the young American ideal ts who concerned themselves with Spain's war favored the other side, that of the Loyalists who wanted land and social reform. Probably the most famous piece of American fiction to come out of the Spanish Civil War is Ernest Hemingway's *For Whom the Bell Tolls*, and its hero, Robert Jordan, fights on the side of the Loyalists. Franco, of course, won. His victory was an extremely disappointing blow to American liberals. Tom would like to have been a part of the struggle, but he was denied that adventure because of his family responsibilities.

As soon as Tom makes the momentous announcement that a gentleman caller is coming, Amanda begins immediately to make plans. As much as she has harped on the subject to Tom, she then begins to question him thoroughly about Jim O'Connor. It is interesting to note that Amanda is more concerned about Jim's drinking habits than she is about the fact that he is a Roman Catholic. Most Southern Protestants had traditionally been strongly opposed to inter-marriages. However, knowing what we know about Mr. Wingfield and his drinking habits, and knowing that Amanda is getting desperate about ensuring Laura's future, it is not surprising that she is careful to make sure that Jim is not a drunkard.

Note also Tom's futile attempt to make Amanda look at Laura realistically. She ignores all of Tom's efforts to evaluate Laura realistically. She refuses to allow Tom to refer to Laura as crippled. But as Tom points out, Laura is more than crippled; she is a girl who lives in a world of little glass ornaments and old phonograph records. But Amanda refuses to recognize this and thinks only that this will be the gentleman caller who will marry Laura.

PART II · SCENE 6

Summary

Tom appears as narrator. He informs the audience that he knew Jim O'Connor in high school, over six years ago. At that time, Jim was captain of the debating team, president of the senior class and the glee club, and he sang the male lead in the annual light operas. A hero to his classmates, he was voted the student most likely to succeed in life. But six years after graduation, Jim is holding a job in the same shoe factory where Tom is employed. He isn't much better off than Tom. It is also revealed that Jim is the young man who referred to Laura as "Blue Roses" in high school.

The scene fades to the interior of the Wingfield apartment. Amanda and Laura are awaiting the arrival of the gentleman caller. The apartment has undergone an amazing transformation. Amanda has worked like a "Turk" and bought a new floor lamp, new curtains, chintz covers, and a pair of new sofa pillows. A colored lantern hides the broken light fixture in the ceiling. Laura is standing in the middle of the floor with raised arms while Amanda makes a few last-minute adjustments on her dress. Amanda is plainly excited by the impending visit, but Laura is trembling with terror. This terror almost becomes panic when Laura learns that Jim O'Connor is the boy she knew and was secretly in love with in high school. She tells her mother that she won't be able to come to the table. But Amanda dismisses her fears lightly and insists that she open the door when Tom and the gentleman caller arrive. She goes into the kitchen, leaving Laura alone, and a moment later Tom and Jim appear on the fire escape steps.

Hearing their approach, Laura hides behind the portieres. Tom has forgotten his key and gives the doorbell a long ring. Amanda marches out of the kitchen and orders Laura to go to the door, which she finally does after playing a record on the phonograph to help sustain her faltering courage. Tom enters with Jim. He introduces Laura, but she is too flustered to do more than acknowledge the introduction briefly and flee from the room. Tom explains Laura's behavior to Jim by saying that she is extremely shy. Jim says that it is unusual these days to meet a shy girl. He and Tom then discuss their hopes and dreams for the future.

Jim's ambition is to become an executive with an important company. He is taking a night school course in public speaking to acquire "social poise," which he feels is a prerequisite for attaining success in the business world. Tom confides that he is planning to make a big move soon, away from the shoe factory and into a world of adventure. He shows Jim his Merchant Marine papers, which he recently received. He also confides that he paid his union dues with the money that should have gone for the electric light bill. At this point Amanda appears in the room to meet Jim. When Tom sees her he is somewhat shocked by her appearance. She has put on an old dress which she wore many years before in Blue Mountain, Mississippi. Her hair is in ringlets and her manner is now coy and absurdly girlish. Tom is embarrassed, but Jim grins warmly and is immediately won over by Amanda's southern charm.

After welcoming Jim effusively, Amanda calls Laura to join them at the table. Laura, who is about to faint from fear, enters the room nervously and moves toward the table. A sudden storm arises outside and the curtains on the window billow inward. Laura stumbles, reaches for a chair to support herself, and moans. Tom helps his sister to the sofa in the living room. Amanda apologizes to Jim by saying that Laura has become ill by standing over a hot stove. As rain begins to fall outside, Tom returns to the table. Dinner begins with Amanda glancing nervously at Jim. In the living room, Laura stretches weakly on the sofa, trying to hold back her sobs.

Commentary

Tom, in summing up Jim O'Connor, seems to see him as just a plain individual. Certainly, during the course of the play, he shows no exceptional qualities. In the next scene, he will be seen as a rather blundering and awkward person.

Notice that a large part of Laura's nervousness and sickness in this scene is brought about by Amanda's constant fretting and bothering. Laura even says to her: "Mother, you've made me so nervous." Again, this shows Amanda's inability to understand her children. This is further emphasized when Amanda tells Laura that "you couldn't be satisfied with just sitting home." In reality, Laura would be quite content to remain home alone—she seems at this point to have no desire to meet other people.

Before Jim O'Connor arrives, Amanda is busy changing into the dress that she wore when she met her husband. Again, it is difficult to know whether Amanda wants gentlemen callers for herself or for Laura. Certainly, she wants Laura to get married, but it will be seen to be Amanda who enjoys the idea of having the gentleman caller. She reverts back to her girlish days in both behavior and dress, and she appears with jonquils, the same flowers she carried the summer she met her husband.

During the course of the conversation, Amanda mentions Mr. O'Connor's name. At this point Laura finds out that it is the same Jim O'Connor she had a crush on in high school, and she tells Amanda that she will have to be excused. But Amanda will have no part of this "silliness." She forces Laura to open the door even though Laura is visibly agitated. Again, Amanda tries to make her children conform to her idea of behavior rather than letting them assert their own personalities.

Notice here the stage direction. As soon as Laura opens the door, she rushes across the room to the phonograph. Her crossing the stage with her limp emphasizes her agitated state. Likewise, her retreat to the phonograph suggests her reliance upon her own world rather than meeting with the new world represented by the gentleman caller.

SCENE 7

Summary

Half an hour later, Tom, Jim, and Amanda are just finishing dinner. Laura is still stretched out on the sofa. Suddenly the lights in the apartment flicker and go out because of Tom's failure to pay the light bill. Amanda, talking quickly to conceal her embarrassment, lights a candelabrum. She pretends to punish Tom for his neglect to pay the bill by making him help her wash the dishes. Actually, she wants the "gentleman caller" to be left alone with Laura. Amanda and Tom go into the kitchen while Jim, carrying the candelabrum, goes into the parlor to talk with Laura. Laura sits up nervously from the sofa as Jim enters. At first she can hardly speak, but gradually Jim's warmth and good humor overcome her shyness. Jim sets the candelabrum down and sits cross-legged on the floor near her. He persuades her to sit next to him.

Jim sees Laura as a girl who simply lacks confidence. As they talk, Laura reveals that she knew Jim in high school. Jim now remembers her as the girl he used to call "Blue Roses." When Laura confesses that she could not talk to him in school because of her self-consciousness, Jim immediately reassures her that lots of people have problems. He goes on to say that many people are disappointed by life. He admits that he himself should be farther along than he is now, but that "being disappointed is one thing and being discouraged is something else." He is disappointed at the way his life has gone since graduation, but he is not "discouraged." He is sure that he will succeed and, in fact, is taking courses in public speaking and radio engineering to help advance his career. Jim's ambition is to enter the new industry of television. "I've already made the right connections and all that remains is for the industry itself to get under way!" he says.

As Jim's enthusiasm mounts, Laura's enveloping shyness begins to dissolve. Jim asks her about her own interests, and Laura shows him her glass collection. She hands him a piece of the collection, a unicorn which she explains is her favorite among the glass animals. Somewhat baffled by Laura's intense interest in bits of glass, Jim changes the subject. He rises and opens the fire escape door. Music from the Paradise Dance Hall comes in. Jim asks Laura to dance with him. He has got it in his mind that she is suffering from an "inferiority complex" and that he, Jim, will instill confidence in her. He has made it clear that her crippled leg is nothing but a small defect which she must learn to ignore. Now, over Laura's protests that she has never danced before, he takes her in his arms and proceeds to waltz happily but clumsily around the room. Suddenly they bump into the table which holds the little glass unicorn. It falls to the floor and breaks. Jim apologizes for his clumsiness, but Laura assures him not to worry. She examines the unicorn, whose horn has been broken off, and says: "I'll just imagine he had an operation. The horn was removed to make him feel less— freakish." She adds that now he will feel more at home with the other horses. They both laugh and Jim is glad to see that Laura has a sense of humor. He then becomes very serious and tells her that she is extremely pretty. He goes on to say that she is different from other people, but that her difference is an advantage: "she is one times one," he says, "while other people are just as common as weeds." He takes her in his arms and kisses her gently on the mouth. Laura, faint with her emotions, sinks onto the sofa with a dazed look, joy radiating from her eyes.

Jim, now embarrassed by his impulsive action, and feeling guilty, explains to Laura that he is engaged to another girl, and won't be able to come back to the Wingfield apartment again. Laura sways slightly under the impact of this news and grips the arm of the sofa. Jim goes on to talk about the power of love, and how the girl he is going to marry has changed his life. The more Jim tries to explain the situation, the more painful it becomes to Laura. She just looks at him, an expression of desolation on her face. Finally, she takes the little glass unicorn and places it firmly in Jim's hand. She tells him she wants him to keep it as a souvenir.

At this point, Amanda comes rushing gaily into the room, carrying a pitcher of fruit punch and a plate of macaroons. Jim announces that he must go, and will not be able to come back because of his engagement. (Jim is engaged to a girl named Betty, a nice, wholesome

American girl who is the counterpart to his dream of "success.") While Amanda is shocked by this news, she bears up bravely and wishes Jim luck, success, and happiness. Jim goes and Amanda calls for Tom. He enters the room and Amanda turns on him angrily. She accuses him of playing a joke on them, of bringing home another girl's fiancé. Tom insists that he did not know of Jim's engagement. After further accusations by Amanda, Tom leaves the apartment to go to the movies—his only escape from his mother. As he goes out of the apartment, Amanda shouts out furiously, "Go, then! Then go to the moon—you selfish dreamer!"

The light dims slightly and Tom appears before the audience as narrator. While he is talking, Amanda and Laura are seen in the living room. The scene between them is played in pantomime. Amanda appears to be comforting her daughter who is huddled before her. Now that the mother's speech can't be heard, her silliness is gone and she has great dignity and beauty. Laura lifts her grief-stricken face to Amanda and smiles. Her mother's speech has comforted her. Then Amanda, after looking briefly at the father's portrait, exits from the room. Tom, who has been addressing the audience during this scene, says that he left home after being fired from the shoe factory for writing a poem on the lid of a shoe box, and that since then he has been drifting from city to city. But try as he may, he cannot escape from the memory of his family. Wherever he goes, he is reminded of Laura. He cannot forget his sister. At the end of Tom's speech, Laura rises from the sofa in the living room, picks up the candelabrum, and blows the candles out.

Commentary

During the first part of this scene, Amanda's conduct does show that she knows how to entertain and that she is not overly distracted by the lights going out. She is also very careful to use this as an excuse to get Tom into the kitchen so as to leave the gentleman caller with Laura.

The scene between Laura and Jim O'Connor gives us our first view of Laura as a person. Suddenly, she comes alive as an individual, unique and different, but with her own charm that goes much deeper than the superficial gibbering of Amanda.

Note that, as the scene progresses, Laura rapidly gains confidence in herself and begins to lose some of her shyness. She relaxes enough to show Jim her glass menagerie, a collection that she treasures and that she would not readily show to just anyone. It is then that she explains her preference for the unicorn, which, like Laura, is different from the other animals; its uniqueness makes it Laura's favorite. Symbolically, the unicorn here represents Laura's own self. She is also different and unique. But she, like the unicorn, doesn't complain about being lonesome or unique and, like Laura, the unicorn is the most delicate of all the animals in the collection.

After looking at the collection, Jim proposes to Laura that they dance. He is still trying to build up her ego and to prove to her that she is not as different as she thinks herself to be. In other words, he is trying to break through to Laura. But the dance is used also as the method by which the unicorn is broken, and Jim's clumsiness can also break the delicate Laura.

As soon as the unicorn is broken, Laura maintains that now it does not feel as freakish and looks more like the other horses. Symbolically, Laura is feeling more normal now than she has ever felt. Even though Jim seems to the audience a rather ordinary young man, to Laura he is quite exceptional, and he has achieved his aim of bringing Laura somewhat out of her world of retreat.

After Jim makes his awkward confession about his engagement to Betty, Laura gives him the broken unicorn. Here the symbolism may be variously interpreted. We may see the broken unicorn as Laura's broken hopes, or we may say the broken unicorn is no longer unique like Laura but instead it is ordinary like Jim; or it may represent her broken hopes for love and romance, and she gives the symbol of her love to Jim to take away with him since he has broken her as well as her unicorn. That is, symbolically he takes away her broken unicorn and her broken love.

Structure

Methods of Analyzing Structure

A play is a story told through dialogue and action. It attempts to imitate reality (reality is here defined by Aristotle as men-in-action). The dramatist presents his story directly to an audience through a combination of movement, sound, and mimetic action. All is contrived to make the audience believe in what it sees and hears. The audience meets the dramatist halfway by pretending that what it sees is, for the moment, real. The audience wishes to be entertained, engrossed, horrified, or enlightened. The dramatist does all these things, but in addition he attempts to disturb the minds of the members of the audience by imitating reality with penetration and insight into human nature. To achieve any of these effects the dramatist must present his story skilfully. The dramatic elements he must manipulate are action, plot, tempo, setting, character, and dialogue.

1. Action

The action of a play consists of several events which relate to each other. Each event is understandable only in relation to the others, yet in itself it has meaning and wholeness. Most events in a play are *outward events* in which the characters do things observable to the eye. Some are *inward events* or mental states, such as likes and dislikes, decisions, acceptances and rejections.

2. Plot

The plot is the arrangement of events so that the relationships of the events become meaningful to the audience. The usual relationship between two events is *causal*. Other relationships, such as *time, place,* also occur. A plot with a strong pattern of causal relationships is called a "tight" plot. A "loose" or "episodic" plot is one in which things happen in a haphazard manner in the same place or at the same time.

The plot has four distinct parts: exposition, development, crisis, and conclusion. Each part has a separate function and must flow into the others so that the construction of the play will not be conscious or obstrusive to the audience.

The exposition is usually at the beginning of the play; it gives the basic situation of the play. It includes the time and place of events, the events leading up to the action of the play, and the identities and something of the personalities of the characters in the play. The exposition also usually sets the tone and atmosphere of the drama.

In the development of the play, the elements established in the exposition are carried through action towards a resolution or conclusion. Generally, the development of the play involves tension, conflict, or predicament.

The crisis of the play is the turning point in it. The crisis is the point the development reaches when something is done that completely changes the basic situation of the play. Out of this new situation comes the final resolution of the play. Most often the crisis comes at an exciting point in the play—a moment of climax; occasionally, however, the playwright may place a crisis at the moment of anticlimax.

The conclusion, often called the *dénouement,* is the resolution of the play. The best conclusions are those that seem correct and inevitable, as determined from the preceding events of the play.

3. Tempo

The tempo is the rate at which events occur on the stage. The dramatist usually varies the tempo in order to emphasize certain events and to avoid monotony. He varies the tempo by the use of long and short scenes, changes of tone, and detail.

4. Setting

The setting is the physical background to the action. This includes time, place and scenery. A properly defined setting presents the reader with the social and historical perspective required for a true appreciation of the work.

5. The Characters

The characters are the agents who perform the action of the play (in a following section will be found a detailed discussion of characterization).

6. Dialogue

The dialogue, of course, comprises the speeches of the characters. It must reveal the tensions of the play and the nature of the speaker. The dialogue carries forward the action of the play.

Questions and Answers on Structure

Question 1.

Does the action of *The Glass Menagerie* consist mainly of inward or outward events?

Answer

The Glass Menagerie is not a static play. There is much action on the stage. The outward events are exciting and come rapidly one after the other. From the opening table scene through the end of the play, the characters on stage are busy. They are doing things, constantly advancing the action. But there is also much inner action taking place — the characters are always reacting to the outward events. The dreamy, nostalgic mood of the play is especially conducive to inward events. We see Amanda's determination to find Laura a husband take root first inwardly, then outwardly. Tom's frustration is exhibited mostly as inner action; for instance, his interest in the Merchant Marine is revealed through a letter discovered by Amanda. Laura's action consists almost entirely of inward events. We see her reliance on her glass menagerie through timid action represent her inner dependence on them. By the end of the play, Laura has engaged in very little outward action. And her final withdrawal into her own private world is the result of her inability and unwillingness to find acceptance in the real world. Of course, any separation of inward and outward events is artificial. The inward events often motivate the outward ones and, likewise, the outward events affect the inward ones.

Question 2.

What kind of plot does *The Glass Menagerie* have?

Answer

The plot of *The Glass Menagerie* is causal and "tight." The events lead to an inevitable and satisfactory conclusion. The play opens with a scene in which Amanda speaks of gentlemen callers and goes through the events leading to Laura's experience with Jim O'Connor, the gentleman caller, in the final scene. Williams does not waste a word, using all his preceding scenes to build causal relationships up to the final one. In this sense, the play is "well-made," that is, it has a "tight" plot structure. But the plot is also "episodic" in that the scenes are separate, distinct episodes. Although the episodes are complete in themselves, they do lead to the conclusion of the play. Thus, we can say that the plot of *The Glass Menagerie* is causal, composed of individual episodes tightly related to each other.

Question 3.

Trace the plot of *The Glass Menagerie* through its distinct parts.

Answer

The exposition of the play begins when Tom opens the scene in his role of narrator. He gives the social background of the play, explains that the play is sentimental and dreamlike, and describes the other characters. Williams, then, has tightly summed up the exposition of the play in a very few minutes.

The development of the play begins when Tom takes his role as a character in the play. Through the action we learn more about the characters and situations introduced in the exposition. Every event in the play is part of the development leading up to the conclusion.

Since the play is a series of episodes, there are necessarily several crises. The first crisis comes when Amanda finds that Laura has not been attending business college. This drastically changes the situation we began with. Amanda must change her plans for Laura. Another crisis occurs when Tom leaves the apartment following his and Amanda's long, loud exchange after she confiscates his book in Scene 3. From this point on, Tom's desire to escape his drab life and heavy responsibilities becomes an obsession with him. In Scene 4, Amanda reveals to Tom that she knows of his plans to enter the Merchant Marine and that she will let him go without complaint, if he will help her to find a husband for Laura. This is another crisis; the issues have become clarified, and both Tom and Amanda are committed to action. In Scene 7, when Jim explains to Laura that he is engaged to be married, we have the final crisis of the play. Jim and Laura have come together briefly, but both must finally go back to their own worlds of illusion.

The conclusion, or dénouement, occurs at the end of the play when Tom is describing the events following the night of the gentleman caller. Amanda and Laura act out a pantomime signifying Laura's final retreat into her fantasy world.

The Characters

Methods of Analyzing Characters

The characters, of course, are the lifeblood of a drama. They propel the action, speak the dialogue, and, if the play is successful, emerge as real people. The following methods should help the student in character analysis.

1. Character Description

Every character analysis should be based on a firm knowledge of what the character is like. It might be helpful to begin any commentary on characters with a description of them. In this brief survey the student should not overlook any of the essential attributes of the characters. He should consider the appearance of the character (his age, his dress, his physical characteristics), the dialogue of the particular character (the way he speaks and what he says), the actions of the character (what he does usually indicates the kind of person he is), the thoughts of the character (if these thoughts can be conveyed directly to the audience or reader), and the opinions of other characters (as long as the student understands that the characters may be biased).

2. Character Development

The way a character changes, or remains static, throughout the play is one of the student's most important considerations in character analysis. The student must understand how the character develops, and why he develops as he does. He must question whether the change is logical or illogical, natural or contrived, typical or unusual. He must decide, for instance, whether Tennessce Williams has prepared the audience for the ultimate development in the character of Laura, and if he has provided Tom and Amanda sufficient motivation for their development.

3. Character Relationships

Every character analysis must consider the whole world of the play. That world is peopled with characters who interact with each other. We learn a great deal about a character when we study his relationships with the other characters in the play; no character can be studied alone. By examining Tom's attitude toward (and dealings with) Amanda, we arrive at a greater understanding of his character. Another method in establishing character relationships is that of contrast. To contrast characters, we decide in what ways the characters are similar and in what ways they are different.

Questions and Answers on the Characters

Question 4.

Discuss the general characterization of the play.

Answer

In *The Glass Menagerie* Tennessee Williams presents three of the most complex and moving characterizations in modern drama. They are studies in frustration. Throughout the play, Amanda, Tom, and Laura are involved in an attempt to communicate. All their hearts are full of things that need to be said to each other, but somehow they cannot express what is in their hearts. Only Tom, in his role as narrator, can understand the other characters. In his role as a character in the play, he is as blind as the other members of the Wingfield family. However, these characters do finally approach an understanding of each other. Nevertheless, because of their own inadequacies, they cannot transcend this superficial understanding into complete awareness.

Through these characters, all three of whom vacillate between the world of fantasy and reality, Williams give us "truth in the pleasant guise of illusion." And this truth is never spared by the illusion. The characters in *The Glass Menagerie* are doomed because they are lost. The characters Williams creates are genuine, and he does not destroy the realness of them by saving them. The success of the play stems from these portraits of life-like characters in a believable and meaningful situation.

The characters are not, however, equally believable or equally successful. The best and most heroic characterization is that of Amanda Wingfield, whereas Laura is the least real of the characters.

One more aspect of the characterization of *The Glass Menagerie* needs to be emphasized. It is the kind of characters that Williams presents that prevents the play from being a true tragedy. All of these people are failures. They are incapable of coping with their dilemmas. The incapacity is internal to themselves. Thus, the play involves pathos instead of purgation. This, of course, is no reflection on the quality of the play either as theater or as literature. But it is important that the play be recognized not as tragedy, but as a mood play concerned with the universals of beauty and love in a society that puts little stock in either.

Question 5.
In a detailed analysis discuss the character of Amanda.

Answer
After a first reading of the play it might be easy for one to dismiss Amanda as a nagging, nosy, shrewish woman, somewhat silly and completely insensitive to the needs of her children. But this is not the whole picture of Amanda Wingfield. She is also a valiant woman whose greatest virtues are those of determination and concern for her family. She seeks consolation in a world of reminiscences about the days back at Blue Mountain when she had seventeen gentlemen callers in one afternoon. Sometimes embarrassingly, she plays the coquette to the hilt, often becoming as lost in her romanticized picture of the past as Laura is in her fragile and tender world of glass figurines. But if Amanda is caught up in the past, she is just as tightly gripped by the present. Amanda is the only character in the play who tries to make a compromise between illusion and reality. She can never escape the

dingy reality of St. Louis in the 1930's. She is the only person in the play who is both practical and determined. It is her efforts that have held the Wingfield family together following her husband's desertion. Her greatest defect is that she does not understand her children. She refuses to recognize that they are different from her, and from each other as well. She does not recognize that they are products of a culture and generation different from her own.

Back in the lazy, frivolous days of her youth in the South, Amanda was very popular. She entertained wealthy gentlemen callers, but impractically married Mr. Wingfield, who worked for the telephone company. In those days Amanda could afford to fall in love with a man endowed with charm and beauty but little concept of responsibility. She yearns for a return to the days when frivolity was appropriate to her social position. Throughout the play, but especially when she is speaking of Blue Mountain and when she greets the gentleman caller, Amanda's language is excessive. Perhaps she is exaggerating her popularity and romanticizing the past, but the important thing is that she is now convinced that the past was how she remembers it. The past is her refuge from the present—it is her source of beauty in the drab present. Although not nearly as passive or fragile as Laura, Amanda is a delicate and refined woman. The dreadful poverty of the Depression and the responsibilities as head of the family have hardened her, but they have not destroyed her beauty.

Throughout the play she exhibits the frivolous side of her nature. She loves to tell the stories of her youth. And although Tom regards this as ridiculous posturing, he plays the game with her because he knows, as Laura does, that Amanda enjoys (and needs) it very much. She likes to play games, such as when she tells Laura: "You be the lady this time and I'll be the darky." She dresses in an outdated relic of her youth and carries a bouquet of jonquils when Jim calls, and she treats the gentleman caller as though he were calling on her.

But she can never totally escape the harsh present. She is trapped in a world in which she must endure the humiliation of charging butter at Garfinkel's delicatessen. She must submit herself to the unpleasant task of selling magazines to her friends. In order to pay for Laura's abortive business college experiment, she has to work in a department store. She must make the "plans and provisions" that result in laying a trap for the gentleman caller. She must force her son to work for $65.00 a month in a warehouse. She does these things that obviously hurt her pride and self-esteem because they must be done, and she is the only person in the family who is capable of doing them.

The play begins with her calling Tom to the table so that they can say grace. She promptly gives Tom a lecture on table manners. In the third scene she scolds Tom for swearing, and we learn that she has confiscated his library because he has been reading what she considers an immoral book: "That hideous book by the insane Mr. Lawrence."

She fears above all that Tom has been drinking, and that his drinking will jeopardize his job and their security. When he calls her a witch, she is shocked and vows not to speak to him until he apologizes to her. In Scene 4, she admits: "My devotion has made me a witch and so I make myself hateful to my children." She is striking back at Tom in that statement, and he contradicts her. She gets him to promise that he will not become a drunkard and that he will help her find a gentleman caller for Laura. In Scene 5, she harps on Tom's smoking habit, but also reveals that what she most wants for her children are success and happiness. When Amanda finds that Tom is considering joining the Merchant Marine, she is sincerely selfless in her desire that he must make certain Laura is protected before he leaves in search of the adventure and excitement he craves. When Tom tells her that Laura will soon have a gentleman caller, she begins making the "plans and provisions" that result in the dinner for Jim O'Connor. During the dinner, even when she finds that the lights have failed because Tom did not pay the light bill, she does not seriously berate him, and the sound of her rich laughter is heard during Laura's encounter with Jim. At the end of the play, when she has seen that her scheme for finding a husband for Laura has been unsuccessful, she tells Tom: "Go, then! Then go to the moon—you selfish dreamer!" She is defeated, but she is not destroyed.

It is obvious, then, that she does not understand Tom. She is puritanical and narrow-minded in her relationship with him. She feels that she must nag him for his own good—and she probably never realizes that she is nagging. She wants him to have her own willingness to sacrifice—but she is the type of person who does not mind sacrificing; indeed, the sacrifices she makes gives her an acknowledged pleasure. She recognizes the similarity between her son and the husband that she loved so unwisely. And she is both pleased and disturbed by this similarity. She loves her son and genuinely wishes him happiness. What she cannot understand is that happiness for Tom is not success and security. She cannot understand that for Tom, D.H. Lawrence is not immoral but is, instead, the prophet of freedom and the fulfillment of the individual.

Amanda's relationship with Laura is much the same as her relationship with Tom. She is concerned for her and loves her very much, but she does not realize the extraordinary nature of her daughter. In the second scene, she confronts Laura with her knowledge of the fiasco at Rubicam's Business College. She is hurt that Laura has lied to her, that they have wasted the fifty dollar tuition fee she earned while working at a department store, and that her ambitious plans for a business career for Laura have been destroyed. But she is also sincerely concerned for the girl. She knows of the awful life of old maids in the South who have no career and no family, and she is genuinely disturbed at the thought of her daughter "eating the crust of humility" all

42

her life. Amanda will not admit that Laura is crippled or in any sense peculiar. She knows that Laura has her own world of glass animals and worn-out records, but she still will not admit that Laura is totally different from other girls—the only differences are to Laura's advantage. At one point, she protests that she realizes that her children are extraordinary, but her realization is only superficial. At the end of the play, when Tom in his role as narrator makes the concluding speech, Amanda and Laura are visible behind the descending fourth wall. The lighting on them (only the candles held in Laura's hand) is very dim, and Amanda is comforting Laura. In the stage directions, Williams describes Amanda at this moment: "her silliness is gone and she has dignity and tragic beauty." This is Amanda's finest point in the play. She is, as always, coping with the situation. Moreover, there is the indication that for the first time in the play Amanda understands and is willing to admit the real situation.

One other side of Amanda must also be considered. She is the prototype of one of Williams' favorite female characters: the aging southern gentlewoman beset by hard times. The "Southernness" of Amanda is somewhat exaggerated by her desire to live in her illusions, now almost a stereotype of southern decadence. She uses her children, especially Laura, to relive her life. In a sense, she thinks that Jim O'Connor is her gentleman caller, not Laura's. The beauty of Laura, although it is unlike her own vivacious beauty, reminds her of her Blue Mountain youth. Tom is a constant reminder of her dashing Mr. Wingfield. Her belief in the horror of alcohol and the idea that Christianity has raised man above his instincts are dominant southern Protestant viewpoints. She reflects not only the genteel and happy aspects of the southern myth, but also the self-righteous and narrow-minded side that Williams indicts as vigorously as he indicts the myth of the "Great American Dream."

Amanda Wingfield is one of the most successful characterizations in American drama. She is truly heroic and many-sided. She develops as the play develops. She is strong and willful, and at the same time she is vulnerable. She must seek beauty and refuge in her private world of the past just as her children seek refuge in their own worlds. She is both practical and romantic. She loves her children, and she is insensitive to them. At the end of the play there is some indication that she has come to an awareness of her problems and the problems of her family. She is not the villainess of *The Glass Menagerie,* although from first reading she might seem so.

Question 6.
Trace the withdrawal of Laura Wingfield.

Answer
All the action in *The Glass Menagerie* revolves around Laura but

she does nothing to further the action of the play until the final scene. She is a tender, moth-like girl who cannot cope with the harsh world. She is somehow "different" in a world that stresses conformity. Unlike Tom, who wants to escape into a more exciting world, Laura does not seek adventure. What she seeks is security in a world where she is not peculiar. That world is the world of her fragile glass animals and worn-out phonograph records.

Laura had to drop out of high school because she failed her tests and was too shy to take them again. She has a slight limp, which is more real than Amanda admits but less noticeable than Laura thinks. She imagines that everyone is aware of her limp and the clumping sound of her brace. (Perhaps the author inflicts Laura with a physical defect because of his reluctance or inability to deal with mental introversion.) At school, Laura was so terribly shy that she would not even speak to her one friend, Jim O'Connor, who teasingly called her "Blue Roses." After she quit high school her mother enrolled her in Rubicam's Business College. The first day she took a speed test at school she was so nervous that she vomited. She could not bear to face her teachers and classmates again, so instead of attending the business college, Laura spent her days walking in the park, visiting the zoo, the art museum and the Jewel Box, "that big glass house where they raise the tropical flowers." She lied to her mother because she could not bear to face the "awful suffering look" on Amanda's face.

On the most obvious level, Laura is extremely naïve. She believes the wild story Tom tells her when he comes in drunk. But from the beginning of the play it is obvious that she notices things and is sensitive to them. She knows that Amanda loves to tell stories about Blue Mountain and she listens to them avidly, even prompting her mother on occasion. But she also knows that she will have no gentlemen callers of her own. She realizes she lacks the vibrancy of her mother. She knows that Amanda and Tom quarrel, and she is hurt by the dissension in the household. During the shouting matches between Tom and Amanda, a light is focused on Laura. Whenever they fight and whenever she herself feels danger or awkwardness, Laura rushes to her stand of glass sculptures or the old phonograph that was left behind by her father.

Laura is as fragile and beautiful as her gently sculpted figurines. Like them, and all beautiful things, she is out of place in the real world. She could never make a business career for herself because of her hypersensitivity and her uniqueness. She is like the blue roses in that she does not exist in a real world. Her world is peopled with the glass animals that are so like her. She cares for them tenderly and protects them from the ugly reality of dingy fire escapes and busy people who have no time for beauty. Also in her fantasy world is her idealized memory of Jim O'Connor, a self-confident, ordinary person who seems unique to her because she herself is so different.

44

It is in the final two scenes that her own particular kind of charm and beauty becomes evident. In the stage direction Williams says: "A fragile, unearthy prettiness has come out in Laura: she is like a piece of translucent glass touched by light. . . ." She does not have the vibrancy or the poise that her mother wants her to have, but she does possess a unique charm and tenderness that the gentleman caller finds enchanting. At first, Laura is too shy even to open the door after she has learned that this gentleman caller is the Jim from her high school days. She fears that the real Jim O'Connor will be changed from the Jim she has secretly idolized for so long. Under the prodding of Amanda she goes to the door, but she is unable even to make conversation and she runs away. She is too upset to eat dinner, so she sobs on the sofa while Tom and Amanda entertain her gentleman caller.

In the last scene Laura overcomes her shyness with help from Jim. She is awakened to the real world and to romantic love. She is very tense—Williams describes the scene as "the climax of her secret life." She tells Jim how much she enjoyed his singing in high school. He is surprised she knows about his exploits in high school and then remembers her as the girl he used to call "Blue Roses." As she speaks admiringly of him, he is flattered. Amateurishly, he tries to psychoanalyze Laura, naïvely feeling that her problem is simply an inferiority complex. Finally realizing how special this girl who worships him really is, Jim is able to lift her, if only briefly, from her interior isolation. However, Jim does not simply transport her into the world of meaningless harshness, he also shelters her with his warmth. And, significantly, he, to some extent, enters her world. But he is no more suited to her world than she is to his. The common meeting is brief. He realizes that although this girl is beautiful and has a great capacity for love and tenderness, he cannot sacrifice his own world of illusions for her. He reveals that he is engaged and will not call again. Laura gives him as a souvenir the unicorn whose horn was broken while she and Jim were dancing. This symbolizes the end of her attempt to enter the ordinary world. The unicorn, unwelcome in the modern world because of its differentness, is similar to Laura. With its difference removed, as if by an operation, the unicorn no longer demands the special place in Laura's affections that it did before. Laura, having retreated into her fantasy world, presumably permanently, is comforted by her mother as the play ends.

Laura is the least successful characterization in *The Glass Menagerie*. She never emerges as a character in her own right. We know little about her except through the stage directions and the speeches of the other characters. We do not identify with her; we can only sympathize with her. Perhaps the reason Laura does not develop into a flesh-and-blood character is that Williams identifies her too closely with his sister, Rose. However, her plight—her quality of being lost—

adds greatly to the pathos that is carefully developed throughout the play.

Laura is the girl in glass whose world is infinitely more beautiful than the real one. She is overly shy, and this shyness is even more striking in contrast with Amanda's forcefulness. Her role in the play is central. All the action centers around her. Her destruction, her final retreat into a make-believe world, is the most touching—indeed, almost tragic—element in *The Glass Menagerie*.

Question 7.

Discuss the conflict between Tom's conception of the poet's role and his feeling of obligation to his family. Is he justified in abandoning Amanda and Laura at the end of the play?

Answer

Tom Wingfield plays a dual role in *The Glass Menagerie*. He is the narrator. The play is his memory. As narrator, he speaks at length about truth and illusion, but in his other role, that of a character in the play, he has little more perception than any of the other characters. He is a sensitive young man trapped by unpleasant circumstances that stifle him.

Tom is the potential artist, the "poet with a job in a warehouse." He feels smothered by his job and by his responsibilities to his family. Amanda's attitude toward the things he is most interested in, literature and individual freedom, is exhibited by her diatribe against D.H. Lawrence, whom she calls insane. Tom is trapped on the horns of a dilemma. As a poet, he is interested in communicating truth. He knows that he cannot present truth until he has experienced it. Thus, his soul aches for adventure and experience. He is tired of seeing excitement on the screen and he feels that something is wrong with a society that gains its adventure only through vicarious methods. He feels that until he can escape the confining warehouse job his potential, both as an artist and as an individual, will never be realized. Because he is an artist Tom feels out of place in the ordinary world. At the warehouse he was greeted with hostility by his fellow workers because he wrote poetry. Finally, as a result of his friendship with Jim O'Connor, Tom has won some acceptance. But he wants and needs more than acceptance. His idea of the poet is that of an adventurer, based on the romantic lives of Byron and Shelley, Lawrence and Hart Crane.

The other horn of his dilemma is his responsibility to his family. Tom loves his family, but he does not fully understand them. He feels that Amanda is silly and ridiculous in her memories of Blue Mountain. Since he knows how much she enjoys it, he will prompt her into telling him and his sister about the day when she had the seventeen gentlemen callers, but he feels that Amanda is out of touch with reality. He resents her nagging him, and he thinks he understands why his father deserted the family. He realizes that Laura is not like other girls her age, but he does not fully understand her either. The final scene indicates that perhaps Laura could have been helped, but Tom has been unwilling to try to help her until he is prodded by Amanda. At the end of the play Tom escapes both the confines of his warehouse job and the responsibilities to his family. But this escape is almost an afterthought, arising solely from having been fired from his job. And the escape proves almost as confining as his life with his family.

Perhaps this lack of moral responsibility can be excused on the ground that Tom is no ordinary person. He knows that he must break away from his family and his mundane existence if he is ever to develop as an individual. But the beauty of the play is that Williams does not allow even this character, with whom he obviously identifies himself, to escape completely the bonds that tie him to his family. At the end of the play, Tom, commenting in his role as narrator on his life after he has left Amanda and Laura, says: "I tried to leave you behind me, but I am more faithful than I intended to be!"

Tom is the eternal dreamer. He knows that he must somehow find a more exciting life, but he also feels a strong bond of responsibility to his sister and mother. He is the romantic trapped by reality. When he leaves—actually, he was almost forced to leave—he takes the most positive action in the play. This positive step, however, seems to have been doomed to the same failure as Amanda's aborted attempts to provide Laura with first a business career and then a husband. Tom was never able to forget his selfishness.

The characterization of Tom is an extremely sensitive one. This is his story, his memory. Tom is forced to act heartlessly. And in the years since the action of the play, he has been plagued by his memory of his family. Although Tom was forced by nature and by his role as poet to desert his family, he cannot be excused. Just as Amanda is not the villainess of *The Glass Menagerie,* neither is Tom the hero.

Question 8.

Discuss the relationships between Jim O'Connor and the Wingfields. Is he really very different from them?

Answer

At the very beginning of the play, Jim O'Connor is described as being an "emissary from a world of reality" from which the Wingfields are somehow separated. He is a rather clumsy, friendly young man—the hale and hearty extrovert contrasted with the serious Tom, who is introverted. His looks and outgoing personality made him a success in high school, but since then he has not achieved all that he and others had expected him to accomplish. His job at the warehouse where he and Tom work is not very responsible, but he attends night school and his ambitions are unlimited. He is optimistic and thoroughly committed to a belief in progress. But he is nagged by self-doubts that are hidden beneath the self-confidence he exudes. Despite his protests to the contrary, he is what he most hates to think of himself as being: an ordinary person. He is hardly distinctive from thousands of simple, well-adjusted, middle class youths. His is a crucial role in the play—he is the gentleman caller that the play anticipates from the beginning. He is the catalyst for Laura's initial emergence from her world of glass figurines and also for her final break with reality.

To Tom, the poet seeking adventure and experience but trapped by circumstance in an unexciting existence where only alcohol and the movies offer excitement, Jim O'Connor is dull and unimaginative. Tom rejects the values which Jim almost religiously cherishes.

To Amanda, Jim is that long-awaited event—the gentleman caller. She is perceptive and knows that he is not like her own dashing beaux, but he does have the "get-up" that she wishes her son had. After years of hand-to-mouth existence in a shabby apartment and with the prospect of a restless son leaving in search of adventure, Amanda sees Jim as the dependable, nonalcoholic solution to her daughter's plight. Her enthusiastic welcome for him, in which she relives her girlhood days in the genteel South, is a measure of her desperation. The aristocratic and wealthy gentlemen callers she entertained are now replaced by the unimaginative, clumsy Irishman whose primary recommendation is his enthusiasm. But she is a practical woman and does her best to impress Jim, vicariously enjoying an escape to her youthful days in Blue Mountain.

To Laura, who is as delicate as her figurines and as out of place in a real world as her unicorn, Jim is awesome. He seems unusual to her because she herself is so unusual. She has idealized him since their school days. She has kept her "crush" on him alive by reliving her high school days through her yearbook. Jim is the only boy she has ever liked. He has become a very real part of her fantasy world and, thus, she is at first afraid to meet him again. She fears that he has somehow changed from the smiling, friendly boy who called her "Blue Roses." His appearance awakens her to a brief joy that is destroyed as casually as it has been initiated.

When Jim arrives with Tom he does not know that Tom has a sister. He is shocked by the girlish vivacity of Amanda, but recovers enough to impress her favorably. Soon, he recognizes Amanda's ploy, but he is genuinely affected by the special fragility and beauty that is Laura's. He is surprised and pleased that she knows so much about him. He brashly attempts to psychoanalyze Laura: trying to build up her self-confidence, he lies about her physical defect. This indicates his simple-minded modernity. He even dances with her and clumsily causes the horn to break off Laura's prized unicorn—the one thing that made the animal unique. That Laura is not upset about the loss of the horn symbolically represents her desire to enter the normal world like an ordinary person. He kisses the girl and then realizes that Laura is falling in love with him. This he cannot face because Laura has made him aware of his own insecurity. He tells her that he is engaged and that he will not call again. Laura, who has been holding the glass unicorn in her hand, gives it to him for a souvenir; she can no longer identify herself with the broken animal. She no longer has either the special animal transformed into an ordinary one, or her hero in shining armor, to lead her into a real world. She retreats finally to her world of glass animals and old victrola records.

Jim O'Connor is not a cruel person and is not stupid. He realizes that Laura is a tender and delicate girl, beautiful in her own way. But Laura is too painful a reminder of his own inadequacies. He cannot preserve his illusion about his being gifted and have Laura too. He needs a relationship in which his self-confidence can be secure. He needs the earthy, middle-class comfort of his fiancée who accepts his values as her own. And Laura is too timid to move toward him, so they come together for only an instant and then he regains his own world in which he is still the high school hero most likely to succeed.

Jim, then, is not really so much different from the Wingfields. Like them he must be protected by illusion from a harsh world that prevents individual fulfillment. He is simpler than they are, however, and his illusion represents bourgeois values.

Question 9.

What effect does the absent Mr. Wingfield have on the characters and the events of *The Glass Menagerie*?

Answer

Mr. Wingfield is a character in the play, although he himself is not present in the play. The memory of him pervades the lives of Tom and Amanda. The phonograph and records that he left behind become part of the exotic fantasy world of Laura. Amanda wears his discarded robe, a touching reminder of her loneliness. And his "larger-than-life-size photograph," which is strongly illuminated at times, dominates the setting of the play. The character of Mr. Wingfield is the pivot around which the characters of Tom and Amanda are revealed more completely. Through their attitudes toward this "telephone man who fell in love with long distances," Amanda and Tom are able to communicate some of their own natures. And it was his actions before the play began that initiated this disintegration of the family that is finally completed at the end of the play. And, of course, his earlier desertion helps to protect Tom's action from the moral consequences it would ordinarily provoke.

Amanda's attitude toward her husband is mixed. She obviously loved the charming, handsome man, but he was only a man who worked for the telephone company. He was not the son of a planter, as was each of her other gentleman callers. Her weakness for this dashing man is evidence of her lack of practicality as a girl. But she blames him for her present humiliating position. During her carefree youthful days when she was secure in a fun-loving, indulgent, and graceful society, it was possible for her to succumb to "charm," the element Mr. Wingfield possessed in abundance. Now she can no longer afford the luxury of frivolity. She is determined that her daughter find security with a husband who does not drink and who is not too handsome. Amanda has had her fill of charm and knows it does not provide security. Interpreting Laura's plight in terms of her own, she is convinced that her daughter needs something more practical than romance. Because of her husband's lack of responsibility, Amanda is forced to the duty of making "plans and provisions." She is deeply disturbed by the likeness between her son and her husband. But she is also pleased. Through her son, and especially through the photograph of Mr. Wingfield, Amanda is able to vacillate between the world of illusion—when she was young, when her husband had only to smile and the world was enchanted—and the world of reality—the uncertain and unattractive present where she must plan and provide for her family even to the point of "trapping" a husband for her strangely passive daughter.

Tom's attitude toward his father is also ambivalent. On the one hand, Mr. Wingfield is the architect of the circumstance that traps Tom into responsibility and a mundane life. Like Amanda, Tom resents his father's irresponsibility and blames him for their poverty. But he cannot help envying his father, who managed to escape. Tom calls himself the "bastard son of a bastard." Tom feels that he and his father are spiritual relatives. Throughout the play he identifies himself with his father. He would like the adventure and excitement he imagines Mr. Wingfield to be experiencing. And although Tom finally does break away from his family just as his father did, he is never able to make a complete emotional escape.

Mr. Wingfield, then, is symbolic of escape and romance. In his photograph he is smiling, and in a very real sense his smile is able to enchant even Amanda. But while Amanda sees him finally as an irresponsible drunkard, Tom can sympathize with his father's search for excitement and experience. Mr. Wingfield has been able to make a complete emotional escape, as evidenced by his cruel postcard from Mazatlan: "Hello—Goodbye." Tom is more sensitive than Mr. Wingfield and he can never escape the emotional consequences of his desertion. Whereas the father exults, the son is forever haunted by an action which was compelled by his individuality.

Mr. Wingfield is not in the play, and the comments concerning him are necessarily one-sided, but it is not unfair to conclude that he is a handsome but selfish individual whose irresponsibility leads to the

disintegration of the family, despite Amanda's effor~ ~
gether.

It is sometimes tempting to interpret Mr. Wingfield in~
Tennessee Williams' father. While the elder Williams was a ~ ~ ~e
and hard-drinking man, he seems not to have been at all irresp~ ~ole.
The resemblance between Cornelius Williams and Mr. Wingfield
should not be overemphasized. *The Glass Menagerie* is a piece of
literature, a work of art. It is not autobiography, although Williams
has relied on personal experience in creating this play.

Question 10.

Who is the central character in *The Glass Menagerie*?

Answer

The three main characters of *The Glass Menagerie* are on stage
much of the time, and a case can be made for each one's being the
central character.

Tom is the most obvious candidate. He is both the narrator and a
character in the play. We therefore see him both in the past and in the
present. It is his play, his memory that we see on stage. As narrator he
presents his points of view. But he controls the action of the play only
when he is outside of it in the role as narrator.

A case can also be made for Laura as the central character. The
glass menagerie of the title is hers. The play centers around her; she is
the pivot about which the action moves. The play is always concerned
with her attempt to come to grips with reality. And at the end of the
play, she is the character who is most explicitly doomed. But she is a
passive girl and does little to further the action of the play. Moreover,
her dialogue is not as lengthy and that of either of the two other main
characters.

It is Amanda who dominates the play. Her case is the most con-
vincing. She is the person who does things, initiates the action. She is
the head of the household. At the end of the play, she consoles her
daughter. She is easily the strongest member of her family. Her dialogue is the most memorable, and her characterization is the most fully
developed.

Perhaps one is more nearly correct in saying that there is no central character, or that all three are central. The whole Wingfield family
is trapped by illusion. Even the strong Amanda is helpless in the world
Tennessee Williams creates in *The Glass Menagerie*.

Meaning

Methods of Analyzing Meaning

To understand the meaning of a work of art, the student must
consider its components. However, the components of a play are not

Meaning Chart: The Major and Minor Themes

	Themes	1	2	3	4	5	6	7
					Scenes			
Major	Illusion *vs.* reality	x				x	x	x
	The need for communication		x	x	x			x
	The destruction of beauty			x				x
Minor	The role of the poet			x	x	x	x	x
	The American Dream				x		x	x
	The impersonality of the modern world					x		
	The clash of cultures and generations	x			x	x	x	x
	The need for meaningful human relationships			x				x

52

ends in themselves. The meaning of the play is understood only when the individual elements in the drama—the action, the plot, the tempo, the characters, the dialogue, and the setting—are synthesized and brought into focus. Only when these various components are considered in their relationships to each other can the meaning, or the general statement the author is trying to convey, be understood. The meaning is the sum of the parts, the final statement that can be made about and from the play.

Theme

The meaning of the play is found by an analysis of the central theme of the work. The theme is the basic idea presented by the dramatist. Often there are several themes; rarely are there none. Since the theme is abstract, an idea, the final test of a play is usually whether the dramatist has effectively made this abstraction concrete and real through the action of the play.

Questions and Answers on Meaning

Question 11.

What does the dramatist have to say in *The Glass Menagerie?*

Answer

He presents several themes, many of them mixed together in various ways: existing as parallel strands, as cause and effect relationships, or as chronological developments. The major themes are the ones of illusion versus reality, the need for communication, and the destruction of beauty. Lesser, but nevertheless important, themes in *The Glass Menagerie* are as follows: the role of the poet, the American Dream, the impersonality of the modern world, the clash of cultures and generations, and the need for meaningful human relationships.

Question 12.

How does Williams express the theme of illusion versus reality?

Answer

All four characters in *The Glass Menagerie* are victims of their illusions, and these illusions cloud reality. Amanda relives her days as the most desirable belle of Blue Mountain. When Jim comes to call on Laura, Amanda seems to confuse things, thinking that he has come to call on her. Her yellow courting dress and her jonquils are a part of this illusion. Her giddy speeches and laughter are that of a young girl entertaining her beau, not that of a middle-aged mother trying to trap a husband for her daughter. The references to Blue Mountain and the "seventeen gentlemen callers" are frequent throughout the play. When things are going badly for her and her children in the St. Louis tenement of the 1930's, she retreats into the comfortable, secure world of her youth, before she made the tragic mistake of marrying Mr. Wingfield. She does not live completely in that world of illusion, however. She does make "plans and provisions." She does get things done. She works to send Laura to business school. When that venture fails, she works to earn the money needed to attract a gentleman caller for her daughter. And the stage directions for the pantomime ending Scene 7 indicate that Amanda, during a time of great stress, does not retreat into her illusions, but stays in the world of cruel reality, comforting her daughter.

The character, Tom, is also a victim of his illusions. He thinks that he will find himself in the world of adventure and travel. Vicariously, he experiences the "adventure" of moving pictures, escaping the drabness of his warehouse job and the discomforts of his home life for a few hours at a time. His great illusion is the belief that his joining the Merchant Marine and sailing to all parts of the world will fill the emptiness that is in him. All of this is related to Tom's conception of the role of the poet.

Tom, as narrator, has lost his illusion. He knows from experience that no amount of travel and adventure will shake the demon that is within him.

Jim O'Connor's life, as common as it is, is ruled by illusions. He was something special in high school. Since then he has been only a shipping clerk. But he has taken a course in public speaking and has been convinced, undoubtedly an easy task, that he is still something special, designed for great things in the future. His illusion is the American Dream.

At the beginning of the play, Laura is almost completely ruled by her illusions; at the end of the play, she has surrendered to them entirely. She sees herself as badly crippled, which in fact she is not. She sees herself as unattractive to men, which Jim disproves. She feels different, as freakish as the little glass unicorn. She cannot fit into the world around her. Her world is the delicate, bright, kind association of her little glass animals, supplied with background music from the old victrola records that her father left. For her, the world outside is cruel. Since she cannot stand and fight it on its own terms, she retreats, enfolding her dream world about her for protection.

Question 13.
What does Williams say about the role of the poet?

Answer
The role of the poet is important in *The Glass Menagerie* because the narrator is a poet and the play relates his attempts to reconcile his role as poet and his role as son and brother. Tom believes that to write well he must experience directly as much of life as possible. The func-

tion of the poet is to report truth; the only way to arrive at truth is through experience. This is a highly romantic concept of the poet, one fostered by the English poets Byron and Shelley, and by the Americans, Walt Whitman and Hart Crane. Tom sees Amanda as a threat to his poetry because of what she does to the book by D.H. Lawrence and because she considers his job at the warehouse more important than his writing. He resents both Amanda and Laura because they keep him at this dull job when he should be travelling and writing. He realizes too late, however, that even a poet cannot escape his responsibilities. He has been more faithful to Laura than he had ever imagined he could be.

An interesting contrast is Mr. Wingfield. He has the adventures that Tom longed for, but he was not a poet, partly because he lacked any moral responsibility.

Question 14.

What is the American Dream, and what does Williams have to say about it?

Answer

The American Dream is the Horatio Alger myth: anybody with average native intelligence can, with proper training and encouragement, accomplish anything he sets out to do—go straight to the top if that is what he really wants and works for. It is the rags-to-riches path that nineteenth-century America seemed to offer. Jim wants to believe in the myth. He wants to think that if he works hard to develop his special ability (and everybody has a special ability, he says), nothing can keep him from being an executive someday. He defines the American system in terms of money and power. These are the only proper things for a man to work toward.

In Scene 7, Jim shows some self-doubt. He knows that he is special, but so far he has not gotten ahead. Characteristically, he does not doubt the system.

Williams does doubt the system. He shows in the play that the American Dream is a myth. There are factors in society that keep most people from realizing their potential—poverty, lack of opportunity, an impersonal world. He is also saying that some people simply are not born with the potential—Jim seems to be one of them; he is actually just a very ordinary young man—and it is cruel to teach them that they are.

Question 15.

How does *The Glass Menagerie* deal with the need for communication and meaningful human relationships?

Answer

The Glass Menagerie is almost a case study in thwarted attempts at communication. Laura and Tom see that their mother's talk of the days back in Blue Mountain pleases her, but they cannot understand the full implication of what she is trying to say to them. Tom tries to tell Amanda what he wants from life—adventure and poetry—but he fails to communicate. She sees his desires as manifestations of shiftlessness and selfishness. Laura tries to tell her mother that she is different, that the world outside frightens her, but Amanda sees only deception (the fiasco at Rubicam's) and a lack of spirit. Jim tries to communicate his dream to Laura; she stands in wonder, but she does not understand. She tries to explain herself to him. For a brief moment, he understands something of her uniqueness, but he is not sensitive enough to understand the full implications of it, and her communication with him is shallow and brief. It is only Tom, as narrator, looking back over a few years, who is able to understand either Amanda or Laura, but then it is too late to communicate.

All through the play, Amanda, Tom, and Laura try to establish meaningful relationships with each other. All attempts fail. The only relationship that is established is the one between Laura and Jim in Scene 7, and it is brief—cruelly but necessarily broken off.

Question 16.

How is the clash of cultures and generations important in *The Glass Menagerie?*

Answer

Even though Amanda lives in St. Louis, she tries to maintain the values of a culture far removed in both time and space. Her concern with Tom's table manners and his personal appearance, her drive to find Laura a gentleman caller, and even her membership in the DAR point up the fact that she is trying to transplant Blue Mountain into this lower-middle-class neighborhood. But it is a world where her son is not the son of a rich planter; he is a $65-a-month warehouse clerk. Her daughter is not the belle of the society season; she is too shy to eat at the same table with her gentleman caller. Amanda herself is not the lady of leisure whiling away her time in garden parties and charity work; she has to sell magazine subscriptions over the telephone, and she has worked in a department store. She tries to maintain the values instilled in her by her upbringing, but she is forced away from them at every turn, and she sees her children growing up without them. In looking for a gentleman caller for Laura, Amanda is forced to accept a young man who is a member of a different culture—a young Irishman who intends to get ahead in the very same impersonal commercialism that Amanda despises, a gentleman caller who got his charm not from being brought up in a genteel manner, but from a night school course in public speaking. In times of desperation, Amanda falls back on this bygone culture, at times to the point of making herself seem ridiculous to Jim and even to Tom. Her past culture is her refuge.

Amanda understands neither her children nor Jim. Part of her trouble with Laura and Tom is that they are different from other people, but the gulf between her generation and theirs is obvious. Amanda cannot appreciate what she considers a decline in morals, as pointed up by her attack on D.H. Lawrence. She does not realize that dating is not the same as it was when she was a sought-after young lady. She tries to interpret Tom's and Laura's problems in terms of her own generation, not theirs.

Question 17.
Discuss the impersonality of the modern world and the destruction of beauty as shown in *The Glass Menagerie*.

Answer
The characters of *The Glass Menagerie* live in a society that does not care about their dreams and aspirations. Laura is fragile and has a strange kind of beauty, which the world makes no place for. Tom is a poet, but his world—the Wingfield apartment and the warehouse—does not care, and it provides no place for him. Jim O'Connor showed much promise in high school, but his world is indifferent to the high school hero. The Wingfield apartment is only one unit of a hive of similar living quarters, each indistinguishable from the other.

Amanda once lived in a world that did care, the world of Blue Mountain just after the turn of the century. She remembers this, and it makes her existence in her present, indifferent surroundings even more cruel.

The theme of the destruction of beauty is emphasized by the fact that Amanda's Blue Mountain days are gone. The heavy traffic outside the tenement jars Laura's glass menagerie from the stand. The beautiful adventures in the movies are only temporary. The theme is developed most thoroughly through the destruction of Laura herself. She creates a world of beauty from the little glass animals and the old victrola records, and she protects it. But Laura herself needs protection. She has the kind of fragile beauty that the modern world has no time or place for. While Amanda lives, she will protect her daughter, but she knows that she will not live forever. Laura must have a husband. Jim—the representative from the world outside—sees and responds to Laura's beauty, but he has to reject it. She is denied his protection. Her final action is a retreat into that beautiful world she has made—a world in which beauty is secure.

Style

Methods of Analyzing Style

Style is the way in which an author presents his ideas. Style, of course, includes many elements. In drama, the important elements of style include dialogue, symbol and tempo.

1. Dialogue

Dialogue consists of the utterances of the characters. In studying dialogue we must be conscious of the diction, or word choice, and imagery an author uses. We should be careful to notice if different characters speak differently or are associated with different kinds of imagery. Often a writer uses diction and imagery to create the atmosphere of the play or to delineate his characters more fully. For instance, the long-drawn-out, sentential speeches that characterize Polonius in *Hamlet* show his pomposity and paucity of thought. The frequent use of witch-craft imagery in *Macbeth* creates an eerie, dark atmosphere.

2. Symbol

Symbols are concrete things which are first of all themselves, but which suggest something beyond their physical beings—often abstract and intangible ideas and qualities. Poets have always used symbols because they often offer a convenient way of expressing complex ideas that otherwise could be expressed only awkwardly (if at all). For symbols to be effective, they must be fairly easily recognizable to the audience and must be natural in the context of the work. An example of a symbol that has long been used by poets is the color, white, as opposed to the color, black. Conventionally, white has symbolized good and black has symbolized evil. From this example another point becomes obvious: symbols are highly subjective and artificial. For one poet a particular symbol may have an entirely different meaning than for another writer. The important thing is that the student be able to recognize the meaning of a symbol within its context.

3. Tempo

Tempo refers to the rhythm and the emphasis of the play. The author varies the rate at which events occur on the stage in order to emphasize certain events and to avoid monotony. Shakespeare often interjects comedy between scenes of tragedy in order to vary the tempo of his plays.

Questions and Answers on Style

Question 18.

How does Williams use dialogue in *The Glass Menagerie* to create atmosphere and delineate his characters more fully?

Answer

The diction assigned to each character tells us much about that character and about the general tone of the play. Amanda, Tom, Laura and Jim each speak in an identifiable and recognizable manner.

Amanda's dialogue is filled with southern rhetoric. It is rich and exaggerated, filled with southern expressions and colloquialisms such as "Honey," "Heavens!" "Gracious!" and "I swear." Amanda's recurrent phrase about gentlemen callers is another example of southern rhetoric. The exaggeration of Amanda's speech is especially noticeable in the scenes in which Amanda remembers her girlhood. In the sixth and seventh scenes there is a perceptible difference in her manner of speech. Here, as though she herself is the young lady about to receive a gentleman caller, her southern accent is much more noticeable; it is as though she has moved from St. Louis to Blue Mountain. Instead of saying "for" or "and" in these scenes, she says "fo" and "an." Amanda's speech is always genteel—it seems out of place in a St. Louis tenement. Williams uses Amanda's diction to create the nostalgic atmosphere of the play and to show that Amanda herself is out of place in the real world, just as Laura is. That Amanda's southern accent should remain after many years away from Blue Mountain is a reminder to the audience that she still clings to southern values and to her illusion of Blue Mountain.

Tom is the poet, and his diction confirms this fact. His dialogue is imaginative and rebellious. In Scene 3, his long speech to Amanda, in which he calls her a witch, is both fanciful and intense. Several other of his speeches throughout the play possess this same quality of intensity and beauty, especially the speech about Malvolio the Magician. As narrator, he speaks even more like a poet. His comments and introductions to the episodes are poetic. His descriptions are imaginative and incisive, couched in simile and metaphor—the tools of a poet. This is especially evident in his description of Paradise Dance Hall and in the final speech of the play.

Laura actually does not say much in the play. Her dialogue generally consists of short, almost breathless sentences. Only in the seventh scene, when she describes her glass menagerie and when she dances with Jim, does her speech become warm and vibrant, and then for only a short while. Laura's dialogue reflects her naïvete and withdrawal. Her soft, shy speech is well suited to her exotic, fragile nature.

Jim's speech is in effective contrast to Amanda's. His diction is that of a person who has taken a course in public speaking. It is warm and friendly, but somehow hollow. He uses the colloquialisms common in the 1930's, complete to the clichés of psychiatric jargon. His dialogue reflects his character. He speaks with the confidence drilled into him by a culture very different from Amanda's. He speaks the cheery, supremely confident, and very shallow dialogue of the man on the go. Only in the tender moment after he has broken Laura's unicorn and when he realizes the beauty and fragility of Laura does his speech become serious and meaningful. But the moment is brief, and when he realizes that he cannot let himself become involved with Laura, he assumes the same hollow, jargon-and cliché-filled speech he had at the beginning.

Question 19.

List and discuss individually the major symbols used in *The Glass Menagerie.*

Answer

There are about thirteen major symbols in *The Glass Menagerie.* They are listed and discussed below.

1. *The Glass Menagerie* — These little animals suggest the beauty in fragility. They must be protected from the harshness of reality. This is the dominant symbol in the play. Laura is of the same character as her glass animals. Williams also suggests that the little animals are cold and lifeless; their world is a sterile one.

2. *The Fire Escape* — The people in the Wingfield apartment are—figuratively—burning. Their only immediate escape is the fire escape which serves as an exit from the apartment. It is in ironic contrast to the high verandas of Amanda's youth, since it is ugly and narrow and looks onto a cluttered alleyway—a product of modern urban society.

3. *Blue Mountain* — This is Amanda's illusion, the gentle, beautiful life she led as a girl. It is her retreat, the only source of beauty in her otherwise drab present life. It represents gentility, culture, and all the values that Amanda cherishes.

4. *The Photograph of Mr. Wingfield* — This picture dominates the Wingfield's living room—and in a sense, their whole life. To Amanda, it represents her tragic mistake, her marriage to the gentleman caller who was handsome and charming, but irresponsible and cruel. Nevertheless, she loved him, and she displays his picture in a prominent place. To Tom, his father represents the adventure that has been denied to him. Mr. Wingfield ran away to see the world, and Tom is determined to do the same.

5. *The Warehouse* — This is where Tom must earn the money necessary to support his family. To him it represents the grinding drabness of corporate indifference. It is everything he despises, and nothing Amanda says can convince him that he ought to work hard there to better himself.

6. *The Movies* — These and liquor are Tom's only escape from the otherwise mundane life that he must lead. He identifies with heroes of the movies he sees, and it is through their exploits that he has the only adventure that he experiences.

7. *The Paradise Dance Hall* — This is the world across the alley,

the illusion of beauty (the mirrored globe) and the illusion of love (the furtive sex acts in the alley) that middle-class man must be content with. Its very name is ironic, since it smacks more of Purgatory than of Paradise.

8. *The Merchant Marine* — Tom sees the life of a sailor as offering him the travel and adventure that he feels he must have. His card in the Seaman's Union is his passport out of the drab existence at the warehouse and the Wingfield apartment. In his last speech, we learn that even the Merchant Marine offered no escape, however, from his responsibility to his family, especially his responsibility to Laura—the memory of whom haunts him wherever he goes.

9. *Rubicam's Business College* — This is the everyday world which Laura cannot enter. She is too shy to feel even partially comfortable there, and she leaves it in favor of the aviary and the hothouse in the park. It is her last attempt to go out into the world, just as the gentleman caller is the last attempt of the world to come in to her. Perhaps the name of the college is intended to recall the Rubicon River, the stream that Caesar crossed when he led his armies toward Rome. "Crossing the Rubicon" means making a decision that cannot be revoked and is therefore applicable to this point in Laura's life—her final attempt to go out into the world, an attempt that fails.

10. *The Gentleman Caller* — He is the symbol of expectancy for the Wingfield family. They have waited for him all their lives. Jim O'Connor also symbolizes the outside world from which the Wingfields are somehow separated. Since Jim himself is plagued by doubts and must live in his own world of illusion, he thus symbolizes the universalities of uncertainty and inability to live in a harsh reality.

11. *Blue Roses* — They are identified with Laura. Blue roses are not found in nature. Like them, Laura cannot exist in a real world. The color, blue, symbolizes an unearthly quality for the playwright.

12. *Jonquils* — The flowers are a vivid yellow and they are fairly common in the south. They are identified with Amanda. They represent her vivacity and her life in the past.

13. *The Unicorn* — The unicorn is a mythological animal. Like the blue roses, the unicorn does not exist in the real world. Because he is unique, he has enjoyed a special place among the animals in Laura's glass menagerie. When his horn is broken, Laura is not too upset. She is sheltered by Jim and her calmness symbolizes her attempt to put aside her fantasy world for the real one. When she finds out that the gentleman caller is engaged, she gives him the unicorn for a souvenir. This symbolizes her retreat into her own fragile world. Since the unicorn is no longer "special," he does not hold the special place among her animals that he once did.

These are not the only symbols in *The Glass Menagerie*; they are the major ones. Tennessee Williams uses many symbols in order to suggest complex ideas indirectly.

Question 20.

How successfully does Tennessee Williams use symbols in *The Glass Menagerie?*

Answer

As seen from the answer to Question 19, Williams uses a great many symbols. Some critics have suggested that he uses too many. These critics think that he frequently uses symbols when he should use dialogue to make his point. Most of the symbols listed in the answer to the preceding question are used effectively. That is, they are fairly easy to recognize in their contexts within the play and they express ideas that otherwise could be expressed only at the expense of much time, causing a break in the unity and continuity of the drama. Some other symbols, though, are not used well.

The religious symbols particularly seem out of place and obtrusive in the play. Several times Amanda is referred to as the Madonna. "Ave Maria" is played and one of the screen legends is "Annunciation." Church candles are used to light the final scenes after the electricity is turned off because of Tom's failure to pay the light bill, and at the end of the play Laura holds the candles before her, blowing them out at the end of the play.

Obviously, Williams either sees religious significance within the play, or is trying to use the religious experience to symbolize similar but secular experience. At any rate, the religious symbolism is unsuccessful. At best, it is hazy. We cannot follow the religious symbolism that Williams presents to a logical conclusion. If we accept Amanda as a symbol for the Virgin Mary, as indicated by the references to her as a Madonna and the music to "Ave Maria," then we must logically conclude that one of the other characters is a Jesus figure, most logically Tom in this case, since he is her son. But the Annunciation legend comes in Scene 5 when Tom announces that Laura will have a gentleman caller. Williams must then be equating the announcement that Mary will bear Jesus to the announcement that Laura will receive Jim O'Connor, thus making Laura the Madonna and Jim the Jesus, or more properly Joseph.

Only the use of the candles is in any way valid. In liturgical churches, the candles are snuffed as a signal that the Mass is over. Thus, the blowing out of the candles signals the end of the play. The principal drawback to this is that the play is not a Mass; although Williams attempts to give the play religious significance, he does not succeed and the religious ending has not been prepared for. The use of the candles is, however, theatrical and very successful in that context. When Laura blows out the candles, Tom gains a degree of freedom from her. Thus, this play which has been a "confession" on the part of Tom ends with forgiveness on the part of Laura. This interpretation, it must be cautioned, cannot be accepted too readily since the religious symbolism is inconsistent.

While Williams fails in his use of religious symbolism, it would be unfair to conclude that he does not use symbols well. On the contrary, Williams generally uses symbols extremely well. Only in a few instances is he guilty of ineffective symbolism.

Question 21.

Discuss the tempo of *The Glass Menagerie*.

Answer

The tempo of the first part of *The Glass Menagerie* is fast. Episode is piled upon episode, leading to the final two scenes, in which the tempo slows. In the first part of the play the tempo is varied by the lighting, the music, and the speeches by the narrator. These elements add emphasis and continuity to the play.

Scene 1 begins slowly with the introductory speech by Tom, but quickly picks up tempo in the fast moving table scene. It ends with music.

The second scene begins as the music from the first scene subsides. The tempo reaches its peak in the episode involving Rubicam's Business College and then fades out with music.

Scene 3 is begun by Tom in his role as narrator. It moves into a quick episode with Amanda on the telephone, dims, and reaches a high tempo in the violent scene between Tom and Amanda. The scene ends with Tom shattering Laura's glass menagerie, Laura's wounded reaction, and Amanda's demand for an apology from Tom. It, too, ends with music.

The fourth scene begins with the encounter between Laura and the drunken Tom, then quickly dims and starts the "Rise and Shine" episode which culminates in Amanda's request that Tom find Laura a gentleman caller. This scene is in rather slow tempo, interrupted by music. Scene 4 ends with Amanda on the telephone trying to sell subscriptions to *The Homemaker's Companion*.

Scene 5 has a rather slow tempo. It begins with Amanda's fussing over Tom's appearance. Tom then steps outside the play into his role as narrator and describes the Paradise Dance Hall. Amanda joins him on the fire escape, and in a slow-moving episode Tom tells her that they are going to have a gentleman caller. The tempo then picks up with Amanda's excitement over the announcement. The scene ends with Tom's departing for the movies and a touching encounter between Amanda and Laura. The curtain falls on the first part of the play.

The second part of *The Glass Menagerie* plays somewhat slower than the first half. There are fewer episodes in the second part than in the first. Part II is dominated by the long scene between Laura and

Jim. The play ends on a low key with Tom's closing speech and
Laura's and Amanda's pantomime.

*Landscapes of the Dislocated Mind in Williams' *The Glass Menagerie*

The dramatic pattern Tennessee Williams worked out in *The Glass
Menagerie*—and one which assured it not only initial but continuing
theatrical success—manifests two significant features: (1) the dramatization of men and women by a display of their fragmented, tortured
psychologies; and (2) the depiction of these characters against a haunting environment which is itself a condition of their alienation and un-
happiness. This dramatic realization of what are essentially *landscapes
of the dislocated mind* constitutes typical Williams theater. The pattern
developed is one Williams consistently uses, though with refinements,
in later plays.

In achieving what in the "Production Notes" he terms "a new,
plastic theater" (Vol I. p.131, *The Theatre of Tennessee Williams*),
Williams adapts to the stage a technique already familiar to modern art
media, especially to fiction and film. The entire play is staged literally
with an actor, Tom Wingfield, who is not only the principal character
but who also supplies the point of view for both events and theme of
the drama. The effect recalls a cinemagraphic montage, with simultan-
eous use of interrelated memories, scenes symbols, and musical motifs.
Tom's presentation is characterized, as he himself says, by "truth in
the pleasant disguise of illusion." The story he stages is not simply an
account of how an individual gifted with poetic temperament is denied
a useful, creative life because of a hostile environment and cruel family
circumstances. And if Tom himself recalls similar modern individuals
who search for self-expression, he is also concerned with reminiscences
that quickly suggest much more than his own quest. Both as a major
character and as a narrator he is unable to construct out of the materials he offers either a coherent or a personally satisfying explanation of
reality. Nor is he able to establish with any confidence a genuine relationship with his family, his environment, or indeed with himself. The
world of Tom Wingfield is clearly that of twilight, memory, and fantasy, from which images and shadows of the past loom threateningly
over the present.

Tom's mode of dramatic presentation is clarified by a definition
of two very different types of thinking. *Directed thinking* is logical in
its verbal formulations and intention, for it is causally linked with the

*By Joseph K. Davis. From *Tennessee Williams: A Tribute*, edited by Jac Tharpe.
Copyright© 1977 by the University Press of Mississippi, Jackson, Mississippi. Reprinted by permission from the University Press of Mississippi.

external world by a more or less direct relationship with what it seeks to communicate. *Nondirected thinking* is spontaneously produced and unconsciously motivated. The former is occasionally referred to as progressive because it is oriented to reality and the demands of reality; the latter, as regressive because it is associated with formulations which have no apparently useful, sensible meanings (e.g., as in the materials of most day-and-night-dreaming). Directed thinking seeks as its object adaption to reality and productions which reality esteems, while non-directed thinking turns away from reality and is concerned with a subjective content often bizarre and unacceptable to the normal modes of human consciousness. Tom's narrative throughout consists of non-directed thinking, a concept that may explain the entire play.

The function of Tom extends beyond any thematic intention to render inner experience of some quality of expressionistic reality. In its dramatic mode and theme, in fact, *The Glass Menagerie* portrays individuals not only fleeing from reality but also wishing to escape time and history. Each of the major characters is unable to accept and live with daily events; and each compensates for this failure by rejecting the present through wish-projection and fantasizing. Unable to live in the present, each character retreats into a time appropriate to his or her individual fantasy. Tom Wingfield cannot endure his home life or his job in the shoe factory and uses the motion pictures as a temporary means of escape. Seeing himself as a poet he eventually leaves home and hopes to find a life as an artist. His sister Laura tries to live in the present, but her crippled body and grim prospects in the secretarial school overcome her fragile sensibilities. She withdraws into her world of her glass animals, and so flees into a no-time of approaching mental collapse. The mother Amanda Wingfield cannot accept life in the St. Louis tenement and returns in fantasies to the past—an earlier period of gracious living on the plantation in Mississippi where, as she chooses to remember, she was surrounded by chivalric men of wealth and fashion who wanted to marry her. Each character is capable only of the briefest moments of realistic thinking; none can sustain anything like a vital relationship with another or with the facts of daily existence.

Not surprisingly, then, the dramatic structure of *The Glass Menagerie* cannot be worked out on the level of direct action. The present is avoided and actually repressed as too painful and monstrous to be faced and accepted. The landscape in which each of the three characters seeks refuge is one within his or her mind. Thus the entire play consists of an interplay of shadow and act—a structural movement which supports Williams' theme of flight from the present time and indeed from history.

Laura Wingfield is both the lyrical and symbolical center of the play. Her shattered sensibility and delicate mental balance compel the only instance of genuine affection and compassion either Tom or

Amanda shows in the drama. Unable to cope with her crippled body or the mechanical routine of the business school she briefly attends, she fabricates a nether-nether world out of the glass animals she collects. Quite literally they offer her the only security, intimacy, and permanence she can find in the brutal environment of her St. Louis tenement. Fragile and artistic, these glass figures, like Laura herself, suggest a world other than the one Williams depicts in the play. They symbolize all the artistry and beauty which to her, and perhaps to Williams, are missing in the secular-urban order of the modern era. In high school Laura attempted unsuccessfully to relate to a fellow student. Her secret beau turns out to be Jim O'Connor, the "gentleman caller" whom Tom brings to dinner. Once more Laura is betrayed, for Jim is already engaged to another girl. The idea of Jim as "savior," suggested by Stein (*"Glass Menagerie* Revisited: Catastrophe Without Violence"), provides a final cruel moment in the play. Laura withdraws completely from the present, defeated by the world around her; she moves into the no-time of her glass animals and thus suffers a devastating mental collapse. Williams offers no "saviors," it seems. Art and beauty are given no way to exist in the world of *The Glass Menagerie.*

In addition to his role as stage narrator, Tom Wingfield emerges as Williams' prototypical "fugitive"—a sensitive, modern individual who is artistic in impulse and temperament. Tom rejects both his present menial job at the warehouse and his mother and her professed recollections of a chivalric heroic past in Mississippi. He can only project his life into the future by means of fantasies as a poet. Tom exemplifies, in fact, two related patterns Williams consistently employs in his plays: (1) a rejection of past and present—both the romanticized past of his southern men and women and the bourgeois everydayness of contemporary secular-urban life; and (2) the Orphean compulsion toward the deeply instinctive regions of sexuality and violence. These areas cluster around what William Barrett in *Irrational Man* terms the Oresteian "Furies," or feminine earth-spirits, who demand a place in a society that is increasingly rationalistic and organized to serve the machine. The older Promethean/Faustian lifestyle of post-Renaissance times, represented in *The Glass Menagerie* by the gallantry and heroic order of the South, no longer are viable. Indeed, Tom cannot accept either as real or as desirable the way of life Amanda challenges him to emulate. The brutal fact of the commercial-industrial state cancels any possible return to such behavior. Caught between past and present, therefore, Tom retreats into fantasies and at last flees the stifling apartment.

Only in instances of wish-projections of himself into the future as poet-artist can Tom relieve the terrible depression and anxieties of his deadly lifestyle in St. Louis. Using various literary allusions—Jim O'Connor, for example, calls Tom "Shakespeare"—Williams reinforces Tom's hope that by means of art he might in time escape the world he now lives in. As a further act of rebellion, he identifies with the father who deserted them some years earlier and, thief-like in the night, at last flees. Yet this act occasions the Angst and guilt Tom clearly admits during his troubled narrative. Survival in today's world, Williams implies, is bought at the cost of these debilitating inner conflicts.

The second Williams theme Tom exemplifies is the Orphean plunge into the life of the body. At one point, Tom exclaims to his mother: "Man is by instinct a lover, a hunter, a fighter, and none of these instincts are given much play at the warehouse!" These activities are markedly predatory, but to Tom they belong to a side of human life repressed by sterile organization of contemporary society. Yet they too must have a place in the full life of individuals; for if they are denied, they will rise in behavior that is ugly and violent. In *The Glass Menagerie* this theme is not treated in great detail; but in later plays it emerges with tremendous force and often with terrible consequences for Williams' men and women. So significant is it, in fact, that some clarification of it here is useful.

The Orphic theme, only foreshadowed in Tom's affirmation of man's beastlike aspects, points to several related emphases in Williams' plays. At one level it suggests the supernal power and role of art and artist. The legendary Orpheus, son of a divine Muse and a Thracian prince, was a master musician who rivaled the Olympians themselves. His lyre enchanted human beings and animals who heard it; it even saved Jason's mariners from despair and the bewitching songs of the Sirens. Orpheus, then, recalls the artist whose music calms and heals; for his incomparable songs purge the weariness and pain of life, uniting all who hear their ethereal melodies. At another level Orpheus alone dares the dark powers of the Underworld in search of his beloved Eurydice, taken from him by the sting of the poisonous viper. So beautiful is his music that the rulers of Hades agree to return her to him if he departs immediately and never looks back. Unfortunately, he looks back too soon upon regaining the world above, and Eurydice, still within the gloomy shadows, is lost forever. But in seeking her he has challenged the fearful depth and so is one who quests for the reunification of body (the animal, sexual body) and spirit (the cognitive, enlightened heights of thought). Orpheus attempts to bring nature and man into harmonic unification. Williams clearly introduces both of these characteristics into his dramas.

This Orphean quest for unification of man's animal and intellectual dimensions through artistic means is a persistent dilemma in Williams' plays. Williams is never able to reconcile the split between man the artist and man the thinker. The body in its full, free life always becomes either a brutal punishment or an agent of tragedy. The Orphic dilemma, expressed by the ancient warning, soma sema (*the body, a tomb*), is one of the consistent mythopoeic themes in Williams' work.

As the half-crazed Maeneds tear Orpheus to pieces, tossing his parts into the river Hebrus, so the heroes and often the heroines in Williams' plays must suffer dismemberment in their attempts to live the full life of the body.

If *The Glass Menagerie* only introduces Williams' Orphic dilemma, later works deal more or less consistently with it. *A Streetcar Named Desire* (1947), for example, rejects as dangerous and damaging the idea that individuals can live exclusively for unlimited self-indulgence, especially sexual gratifications. At the same time Williams recognizes that in attempting to seize their lives men and women experience definite limits. Each of us, after all, is not simply situated in this universe; and Williams undertakes specific explorations in his dramas of the 1950s of what moral order, if any, exists. In these plays he examines the terms whereby individuals may purposively act and thus the standards which can effectively measure their actions as creative or destructive. These plays reveal that Williams' investigations are undergirded by the conviction, never entirely absent from his work, that limits exist beyond which persons may not venture except at supreme risk and perhaps inevitable retribution.

That Williams came to such a view of human existence is seen in a growing preoccupation in the works of the 1950s and later with the problem of moral guilt and the violence which all too frequently this guilt generates. In *Camino Real,* a radical reworking of a 1947 play, *Ten Blocks on the Camino Real,* and in *Orpheus Descending,* also a completely reworked version of a 1940 play, *Battle of Angels,* he gives us characters who express what Williams himself terms, with reference to the earlier play, "the romantic nonconformist in modern society" (as quoted in Donahue, *The Dramatic World of Tennessee Williams,* p.58). Both Kilroy in *Camino Real* and Val Xavier in *Orpheus Descending* attempt to live in this world by their own individualistic codes of behavior. Each would realize his life in ways personally satisfying, but at the same time each would act outside the social and moral order of his particular environment. In the end each is frustrated: Kilroy becomes a personification of sterility and thus is thrown into a kind of hell; Val is rendered literally impotent by a murderous act of physical castration.

The dilemma of Williams' Orphean hero is further explored in the controversial treatment given to the martyred homosexual Sebastian Venable in *Suddenly Last Summer* (1958) and in the portrait of the defrocked clergyman Shannon in *The Night of the Iguana* (1961). Despite Williams' clear dramatic presentation of ways in which both these heroes suffer and are punished, we are never quite sure that they themselves are entirely to blame or in fact deserve what happens to them. The framework of the problem of moral guilt is ambivalent; and Williams' handling offers us no easy access to his own views. The theatrically successful plays, *Cat on a Hot Tin Roof* (1954) and *Sweet*

Bird of Youth (1959), for example, may be regarded as instances in which moral guilt brings pain and suffering, perhaps justifiably in the cases of Brick Pollitt and Chance Wayne. We may be entirely correct to say that for Williams man is finally a sinner and that through suffering he must expiate his sin and lose his guilt, but it is far too easy to pass over these complex dramatic presentations with such remarks.

It is more likely that Williams' dramatiziations of the problem of guilt and moral ambiguity contain no successful way out. Indeed, his Orphean hero has necessarily become something of an Oresteian hero—a representative modern individual driven by self-admitted guilt and obsessive fears but who has a deep-felt longing to experience a redemptive vision and win back his peace of mind. Unlike Aeschylus' hero, Williams's hero is yet pursued by the Furies; thus far no divine intervention has occurred to save him and cleanse his tortured soul.

These ambiguities clearly emerge in Williams' delineation of Tom Wingfield and the dramatic pattern of *The Glass Menagerie*. But if Tom is the narrator and central character of the play, the pivotal figure is the mother Amanda; for she is instrumental in bringing her two children to such a desperate situation. She has consistently indulged in illusions and failed completely to meet life directly; and her bitter disappointments have left her impotent, as both adult and mother. Amanda's response to life generates devastating consequences for her children, crippling them psychologically and seriously inhibiting their own quests for maturity and self-realization.

From the opening scene of the play she constantly reminds everyone that she belongs to an earlier time on her family's plantation in Mississippi. As she exclaims to Tom and Laura: "One Sunday afternoon in Blue Mountain—your mother received—*seventeen!*—gentlemen callers! Why, sometimes there weren't chairs enough to accommodate them all. We had to send the nigger over to bring in folding chairs from the parish house." These gentlemen callers were, as she never tires of saying, "some of the most prominent young planters of the Mississippi Delta—planters and sons of planters." A woman was secure in this past time, Amanda thinks, for it was an age of chivalry and elegance. It was a time characterized by what she calls "the art of conversation" and by young ladies "possessed of a pretty face and a graceful figure" and also "a nimble wit and a tongue to meet all occasions." All too sadly, however, it is a time now irrevocably lost. Later in the play she tells Jim O'Connor, the gentleman caller of the present: "Well, in the South we had so many servants. Gone, gone, gone. All vestige of gracious living! Gone completely! I wasn't prepared for what the future brought me." Her admission that she "wasn't prepared for what the future brought me" is, of course, an explanation of her present need to live in the past by means of fantasizing: she deeply believes that she belongs to this earlier age of aristocratic life, not to the grinding daily routine of her St. Louis tenement.

Amanda Wingfield's past not only animates but also sustains her in the present, becoming in effect her point of reference for everything connected with goodness, truth, and reality. She is simply unable to break out of the framework of her dreamy recollections and to achieve any degree of perspective on them as real or imagined elements. She makes invidious comparisons between her former life and her current situation, and she emphatically rejects the present in favor of the past. Her instability is frighteningly apparent in her inability to sustain a relationship between her almost lucid moments of realism and her constant fantasizing. She vacillates from urging Laura and Tom, on the one hand, to prepare for the gentleman callers she believes are about to arrive to warning Laura, on the other, that she must get training for a business or a professional career. Amanda warns that she has seen "such pitiful cases in the South—barely tolerated spinsters living upon the grudging patronage of sister's husband or brother's wife!— stuck away in some little mousetrap of a room—encouraged by one in-law to visit another—like birdlike women without any nest—eating the crust of humility all their life!" These instances of grim realism are unfortunately rare with Amanda; she usually persists in fantasizing about the past and projecting its remembered images upon her present circumstances.

On the all-important evening when a gentleman caller finally appears, Amanda indulges in the consummate fantasy. Entering the room wearing "a girlish frock of yellowed voile with a blue silk sash," she proudly announces: "This is the dress in which I led the cotillion. Won the cakewalk twice at Sunset Hill, wore on Spring to the Governor's Ball in Jackson!" The triumph of the past is seemingly now complete, for Amanda has regressed in her fantasizing to the years of her youthful innocence as a "southern belle."

The past replaces the present; illusion overcomes reality, yet cannot reverse events. In the following scenes Jim O'Connor, the gentleman caller, is only, as Williams himself warns, "a nice, ordinary, young man" who works with Tom at the warehouse. As Laura's former high school idol, moreover, he occasions her final withdrawal from reality. When he confesses he is soon to marry a young girl he has courted for some time, all illusions are shattered. The play ends with Tom determined to leave home and go to sea, with Laura completely crushed and "huddled on the sofa," and with Amanda trying to comfort her. Williams seems to suggest in his closing stage directions that Amanda gains a degree of "dignity and tragic beauty" by her act of comforting Laura; but audiences may find it difficult to accept this assessment. It is perfectly in character for Amanda to assume a role that is only another of the bad games she constantly plays. Regardless of the individual interpretation of the ending, the play clearly shows the destructive, tragic consequences of Amanda's fantasizing, the results of which are only too apparent in the lives of Tom and Laura.

The outcome of events in *The Glass Menagerie* dramatizes the tragedy of indulging in the kinds of behavior and thinking that negate the possibilities of living fully and honestly in the present. Laura is no doubt the individual who shows the deepest personal ravages of these cruel scenes, but Amanda is still the best illustration of how such a mental condition works its corrosive destruction. Not only does she deeply and permanently injure her children but she herself is a victim of an illusory way of life—that generated by her beloved plantation South. The very nature of this civilization and her relationship to it have created in her habits and attitudes which encourage fantasies and illusions. To understand Amanda and the South, we must explore precisely what her southern background means and how its environs have fostered in her such romantic notions and wistful ideas.

The South that we encounter in *The Glass Menagerie* through Amanda's recollections is actually a pseudo-history of the region and thus a kind of myth. It is, however, a particular myth that is highly significant for Williams and for his men and women, since it functions as a mediating image by means of which his dramatic characters understand and measure their lives and current situations. Certain major characters in all of Williams' works are trapped within a mode of thinking oriented to the past, to a psychological impulse to withdraw into a fabricated ''lost'' time. The present exists for these men and women only to the degree that it can be verified by constant references to the past. And the most important of his representations of the past is that of the American South, with its special commitment to a ruined former time and to a haunting awareness of a paradise now lost. In those works which develop themes and characters out of the South, beginning with *The Glass Menagerie,* Williams employs the South of history and myth as an image that mediates between what is and what might be, and thus between life caught as human expectation, desire, anxiety, and life actually realized as human creativity and individual fulfilment. Whether in memory or in fantasy, it animates and informs the consciousness of his dramatic characters, drawing them back ceaselessly into themselves and finally into some sense they have of their relationship to the past.

Elsewhere . . . I have argued that in the popular imagination both the ante- and the post-bellum South are aspects of the American dream of the creation of a new world and the emergence of a new man who will in time bring forth a new Golden Age. The relationship between the American dream and the South, if crucial, is not actually difficult to establish and trace. According to the widely accepted view of southern history, the Old South is believed to have become, soon after settlement in the sixteenth century, a cultural region dominated by manorial plantations graced with beautiful ladies and guided by elegant gentlemen of noble birth and heraldic virtues. Despite the fact that the educated and better informed have always understood the fundamental inaccuracy and romantic idealization of this view, the illusion that the area was a land of nobility and courtly manners persists, largely untarnished by events and time. It is yet argued, in fact, that the South which fought the Civil War was, as W.J. Cash said thirty-odd years ago in *The Mind of the South,* "home of a genuine and fully realized aristocracy, coextensive and identical with the ruling class, the planters" (p. 4). The second view, and a corollary of the first, is that the Civil War and the thirty years following saw the destruction of civilization in the Old South, with the result that except for scattered and isolated remnants the entire structure, with its splendid men and women and its cultivated way of life, disappeared, only to be replaced by a new order of life derived from the powerful commercial and industrial interests then working to transform all of America into a modern technological nation. The Old South remains only in memory; and there it endures today, to serve in its principal features as the idealized model for worthwhile imitation and future approximation.

This account of southern history is hardly credible; it is nevertheless a very important account of the region, embodying a view of the past commonly regarded as essentially correct and true. Actually the Old South of the popular mind is best regarded as myth—but a myth vital and important in grasping the spirit of this geographical region and in seeing its relationship to its own history and to the rest of the United States. As myth this account of the South has exactly the function which Mircea Eliade in *Myth and Reality* (p. 5) explains as "sacred history"; namely, the transformation of the origins and development of the region—from its settlement and colonization to its deep frustrations over Negro slavery and complete defeat in war—into a rendition of its history that is mythic in form and intention. In barest outline, the Old South emerges as an almost idyllic agricultural society of genteel people and an aristocratic way of life, exemplary in its pattern and content. A visionary moment of the American dream occurred and passed; now its history is transformed into the story of a fallen order, a ruined time of nobility and heroic achievements that was vanquished and irrevocably lost. In this way the actual facts of the Old South have been translated by myth into a schemata of the birth, the flowering, and the passing of what others in an earlier era might well have called a "Golden Age."

The significance of the Old South understood as myth is considerable and far reaching in implications. It is above all a kind of pseudo-history accepted as genuine history, and thus as a view of the past by which many people—foreigners as well as Americans—orient themselves in their attempts to comprehend and relate to the American experience. Reliable, accurate history is one thing and myth quite another. History provides the living context to which man turns, to discover not only himself but also his world. There always exists a vital

72

way in which man himself and his emerging life are created by the fact of his being in and of history. At this junction of man and history in their mutually creative union the dynamics of historical consciousness become important. Indeed, for the individual's own continuity, and for his own deep need to experience himself defined within some grasp of origins and the spirit of his own time, he must possess a reliable historical consciousness. It becomes not merely a necessary condition of his full existence in time but also something which takes on the power of a faculty by which he is able to come into possession of his own life and thus to seize, if he can, his possibilities in relationship to himself and his environment.

To find oneself with a largely inaccurate and faulty historical consciousness is to be condemned to a marginal, inauthentic existence. Such an individual is all too likely to be delivered over to those basic impulses we associate with man's bestial life. He is also subjected without aid or relief to those doubts and fears which rise from shadowy suppositions and ancient superstitions. The late German philosopher Karl Jaspers in *The Origin and Goal of History* speaks to this point with great persuasion: "If no ground is firm enough to stand on—if there is no echo for authentic selfhood—if there is no more respect because masks and wrappings do not command respect, but only make possible fetishistic deification—if men do not bring me to an upsurge through the hidden demand of their selfhood speaking out of their existence—then the troubled mind grows into the despair that was prophetically lived through by Kierkegaard and Nietzsche and that attained its most lurid expression in their interpretations of the epoch" (p. 99). A properly functioning historical consciousness grounds one in the present, in real-life activities and situations, and thus in a definite time and place. It "authenticates" man's existence, as if by means of what Jaspers calls an echo (*Widerhall*), by generating an awareness in him of who he is and what and where he is. Without a reasonably accurate historical consciousness, one is confused and bewildered; a faulty, distorted view of history frequently leads one into tragic illusions and even into utter personal darkness (see Jaspers, pp. 231-33).

The relationship between actual history and the way an individual looks at history is important in the successful rise of the myth of the Old South. By the middle of the nineteenth century the southern dream of empire had come painfully to grief. And by the ending decades of the nineteenth century the Southerner began to withdraw into an insular view of his region and its heritage. The still unrealized demands of the Negroes for justice and some measure of human equality, as well as the mounting tensions caused by the rapid industrialization and urbanization of the Old Confederacy, contributed significantly to the impulse to retreat into the legacy of the southern past. Now, however, the order and achievements of that earlier time are fully translated into the myth of the Old South. This tendency is only another instance of projecting on the recent past what are actually wish-fantasies of the present—here, a yearning for recovery of a lost time now transformed by means of a pseudo-myth into a marvellous and heroic era associated with the idea of a Golden Age. As a kind of history the myth will serve as deeply revered consolation and refuge for the white Southerner as he struggles with the actual heavy burdens of his daily situation and as he lives with the sharp consciousness of his defeated, ruined dreams.

The image of the South contained in *The Glass Menagerie,* as indeed in all of Williams' southern plays, is neither accurate history nor proper myth. What we are given in both cases is a falsification of history and a distortion of myth. That is, the South portrayed in Williams' works is an instance of how the popular imagination rewrites history and counterfeits myth, doing so largely out of a mentality that is incapable of handling the actual situations of life and thus of working through difficulties to establish a creative relationship between the past and the present. According to Nancy Tischler (*Tennessee Williams: Rebellious Puritan,* pp. 1-3), Williams himself apparently accepts this mythopoeic reading of southern history. Certainly the image of the South he employs brilliantly serves his dramatic purposes. Unable to confront and accept their present lives, his characters are in desperate flight from time and actual history—literally, from a defeated present and thus from their fears of what they have become. None takes responsibility for his or her acts, and none is able to achieve an authentic, creative life. Trapped in time past or time future, each falls victim to illusions, illnesses, fantasies, violence—or, worse— to definite kinds of insanity. Such then are the results of repression and attempts to avoid contemporary situations.

The best dramatization of what a false historical consciousness means to an individual is Williams' portrayal of Amanda Wingfield in *The Glass Menagerie.* The view she holds of her own origins and early life in the South—or, specifically, that wistful remnant of the Old South surviving in recollections of her home at Blue Mountain, Mississippi—is so distorted by illusions and fantasizing that her integrity and character have been thoroughly undermined. The prototype of all Williams' southern women, Amanda is directly responsible for the terrible and permanent alienation of Laura and Tom. Because she herself has withdrawn from reality, preferring rather dreams of a lost time in the South, Amanda has handed her children over to a similar, if not a worse, psychology and grim fate. *The Glass Menagerie,* in effect, gives us Williams' poignant dramatization of the dreadful human waste of illusions. The major characters in this play are so warped and their lives so distorted and perverted by fantasies that each is left with only broken fragments of what might have been.

Seen in its larger implications, the image of the South, whether approached as history or as myth, constitutes the ultimate landscape of the dislocated mind for Williams' characters. It is not merely the vital context in which his men and women exist; it is for them a final possible "environment"—the extreme of their psychological fantasies—for it must somehow provide them with the means to establish values and to measure the possibilities of life. We are hardly surprised when bitter frustrations and violence result from their efforts.

*The Glass Menagerie:
"It's no tragedy, Freckles."

At the opening of The Glass Menagerie, Tom comes out of the shadows of the Wingfield apartment, the stage magician promising to explain the tricks in his pocket. But Tom is a creature of the shadows who never really admits what he has up his sleeve. He says "the play is memory"; it is also forgetting. In another version of The Glass Menagerie, the story called "Portrait of a Girl in Glass," the narrator is more honest about what he remembers: "In five years' time I had nearly forgotten home. I had to forget, I couldn't carry it with me" (One Arm, p. 112). That is what Tom would say too, except that he has been unable to shake his memories of home because his sister will not be forgotten: "Oh Laura, Laura, I tried to leave you behind me, but I am more faithful than I intended to be!"

In this "memory play" Tom remembers in order to forget. The contradiction in terms can be explained by the double game Tom is playing in the theater as "the narrator of the play, and also a character in it." He is inside the illusion that he calls "truth in the pleasant disguise of illusion," and he is on the outside, "an emissary from the world of reality." In his first appearance, already dressed as a merchant sailor, Tom seems safely outside. But he is still haunted by the memory of his sister, still searching for anything that can relieve his feelings of guilt, "anything that can blow your candles out!" The intention of The Glass Menagerie is to leave Laura in the past, in the shadows on the other side of the scrim, to plunge her "into everlasting darkness." The shadows fall across the stage after Tom uses the money for the light bill to pay his dues to the merchant marine; and at the end when he directs Laura to blow out the candles, the darkness is complete. Tom has to re-enter the past a final time, to make a play out of his memory, in order to leave memory behind. Once Laura, as a character in the play, can be brought to forgive and forget Tom's running away, he can make good his escape.

From the first moment he enters the play, Tom is trying to escape. He no sooner comes to the table than he pushes away because Amanda

*By Thomas E. Scheye. From Tennessee Williams: A Tribute, edited by Jac Tharpe. Copyright© 1977 by the University Press of Mississippi, Jackson, Mississippi. Reprinted by permission from the University Press of Mississippi.

is carping at his table manners, and he plays most of the scene while standing at the portieres. Like the transparent scrim, the portieres curtain off an inner stage; they are another dividing line between illusion and reality or one kind of truth and another. According to Williams' stage directions, Amanda addresses Tom as if he were still at the table, and Tom answers her. Otherwise, "he plays the scene as though reading from a script," motioning once for music and then for a spotlight on Amanda. Tom is divided between two roles: the actor inside the illusion and the narrator or playwright on the outside. From the start he is trying to keep his distance. And his direction is clear: he is on the way out.

Scene three, which opens with Tom's soliloquy on the fire escape, closes with his making his move to escape. This time it is not Tom's table manners that provoke the quarrel with his mother, but his writing, Amanda's "interruption of Tom's creative labor." There is a contradiction between what Tom is doing and what he dreams of doing, between the day job which ties him to the apartment and the nightly creative labor which demands his freedom. "I'm leading a double-life," he tells his mother, "a simple, honest warehouse worker by day, by night a dynamic *czar* of the *underworld*." The foolishness here hardly disguises the terms of the conflict; it is the same conflict as between his two roles in the play. Either Tom stays inside, working for the Continental Shoemakers to pay the rent on the apartment, or he runs away to the merchant marines, gets free to write his play. And that course is threatening to the Wingfields.

After threatening to explode all their illusions Tom charges for the door. When he is caught up in his coat and throws it off, striking the shelf where the glass collection is, "there is a tinkle of shattering glass. Laura cries out as if wounded." Tom is drawn back into the room, into the world of the glass menagerie, in an attempt to comfort her. The symbolism, which is obvious without being a nuisance, states the predicament: Tom cannot escape until he finds the way to leave without shattering Laura's fragile self.

That is a trick he learns from the stage. At the movies' stage show the headliner was Malvolio the Magician—Tom came out of the audience to help him—and the magician proves to be his savior. Malvolio can turn water into wine, and triples the miracle of the wedding feast by turning the wine into beer and the beer to whiskey. "But the wonderfullest trick of all was the coffin trick. We nailed him into a coffin and he got out of the coffin without removing one nail. . . . There is a trick that would come in handy for me—get me out of this two-by-four situation!" In *The Glass Menagerie* the sorcerer's apprentice becomes the stage magician. He brings home a conjuring scarf which he gives Laura as a "souvenir," something to remember him by. And it is a conjuring trick—turning Jim O'Connor into a gentleman caller—that will solve Tom's predicament.

Tom conjures up Jim O'Connor as his surrogate after Amanda agrees that once "there's somebody to take your place," he is free to go. Turning Jim O'Connor into the gentleman caller turns the trick because he can do what Tom could never do by himself: get out of the two-by-four situation without removing one nail. Jim deserts Laura and she is not shattered by it; in fact she is able to say, "It's no tragedy."

Tom offers no reason why the incident with the gentleman caller should be his cue to leave, but Jim's identification with Tom provides a clue. Like Tom, Jim leads a double life, by day and night. Or, as he puts it more prosaically, "I have a couple of time-clocks to punch. . . . One at morning, another one at night." In the world of the play, he is as much a contradiction as Tom, both inside and outside the illusion. Tom captures the contradiction when he describes the gentleman caller in the opening monologue as "the most realistic character in the play" and also a symbol. He is Tom's friend at the warehouse and the playwright's personal symbol. Tom calls him "an emissary from a world of reality that we were somehow set apart from." But it is precisely from that world that Tom returns in scene six, to usher in the gentleman caller. The acting edition of *The Glass Menagerie* specifies that Tom is dressed as a merchant sailor for the monologue in scene six as he is at the opening and close of the play.

The gentleman caller is "the long delayed but always expected something that we live for." All the Wingfields are living for the day he comes to call. "Haven't you ever liked some boy?" Amanda asks; Laura has never stopped loving Jim. Williams describes Laura's scene with the gentleman caller as "the climax of her secret life." He is what Amanda has wished for on the "little silver slipper of a moon" rising over Garfinkel's delicatessen and what Tom has wished for too.

Jim O'Connor is "A nice, ordinary young man" who is transformed, as if by magic, into the romantic figure of a gentleman caller. Tom refers to this image as an "archetype of the universal unconscious," "this spectre, this hope"; he is drawn not from life but from the "serialized sublimations of ladies of letters" in the magazines Amanda sells over the phone. The sort of gentleman caller Amanda herself had known once has died out or disappeared; in the violence and confusion of the thirties, the world "lit by lightning" instead of candles, he no longer exists except in books — or plays.

Jim O'Connor seems the unlikeliest choice to fill the role. He is a great believer in the importance of the "right connections," the power of positive thinking, and the virtues of a night school course in public speaking. He is confident that "social poise" allows anyone to hold his own on any social level; he even tries to sell Laura on his own naive faith in "the cycle democracy is built on." All men are created equal, everyone is just like everyone else, only better: "Why, man alive, Laura! Just look about you a little. What do you see? A world full of common people! All of 'em born and all of 'em going to die! Which of them has one-tenth of your good points! Or mine! Or anyone else's as far as that goes—gosh!" But as he becomes aware Laura is truly different, he turns into something surprisingly different too. Under the spell of Amanda and her jonquils and romantic candlelight and the strains of "La Golondrina" he emerges as an emissary not from the world of reality but from Blue Mountain. When he observes that Laura's principal trouble is "a lack of confidence in yourself as a person" and tries to convince her to "think of yourself as *superior* in some way," he is using the words he has learned will make friends and influence people. When he asks Laura to dance, he is fumbling for the accents of the spectral gentleman caller: "Or is your program filled up? Let me have a look at it. . . . Why, every dance is taken! I'll just have to scratch some out. . . . Ahhh, a waltz!" And to the music from the Paradise Dance Hall he waltzes her uneasily around the room.

It is during their dance that the unicorn is knocked to the floor, the second time in the play that something from the glass menagerie is broken. The first time, Laura cried out as if she herself were wounded; now she can say, "It doesn't matter." All the figurines are part of Laura's own little world, but the unicorn is different, as Laura is different. It is, she says, her favorite of the glass menagerie; given the playwright's "weakness for symbols," the unicorn can be identified with Laura. And yet she can say, "It's no tragedy, Freckles," calling Jim by a special name.

In "Portrait of a Girl in Glass," Freckles is a character in a book that Laura reads over and over, "actually lived with." When Jim comes to dinner Laura mentions his freckles, and Jim says Freckles is his nickname. "She looked toward me," the narrator says, "as if for the confirmation of some too wonderful hope. . . . Yes, he had undoubtedly assumed the identity—for all practical purposes—of the one-armed orphan youth who lived in the Limberlost, that tall and misty region to which she retreated whenever the walls of Apartment F became too close to endure." But Jim's identification with the gentleman caller, and Laura's with the unicorn, are broken after the horn is broken.

Losing the horn, Laura thinks, is a "blessing in disguise" because it makes the unicorn less freakish, more like the other horses. "I'll just imagine he has an operation," she says. The line takes on nightmare proportions if the breaking of the horn is taken to symbolize Williams' own sister Rose's prefrontal lobotomy. But Rose's fate is not Laura's. By his stumblejohn gallantry Jim teaches Laura to have some confidence in herself, shows her that she is different from other people and should stay that way—even if it means never moving from the shelf, being left alone. It is the gentleman caller who speaks: "The different people are not like other people, but being different is nothing to be ashamed of. Because other people are not such wonderful people.

They're one hundred times one thousand. You're one times one! They walk all over the earth. You will just stay here. They're common as—weeds, but—you—well, you're—*Blue Roses!*"

Jim makes the final romantic gesture when he sweeps her up in his arms to kiss her. And having kissed her he takes leave—but not before she presses the broken unicorn on him as "A—souvenir." Since it is "just like all the other horses" now, it belongs in the world of reality where Jim lives; Laura does not. The unicorn is a painful reminder of what might have been but had better not, something for him to remember and for her to forget: the dream of ever liking some boy or ever having a gentleman caller.

Jim O'Connor has played the role in which he was cast, and played it well by playing it badly. His impersonation of a gentleman caller is so clumsy that Laura can see the apparition for what it is. And perhaps she sees that if her dream did come true, come to life, he might look like Jim O'Connor, he would not be made of glass and he could crush her fragile existence as he had broken the unicorn. And so she can say, "It's no tragedy, Freckles."

Tom's leaving her is no tragedy either; at least Tom can convince himself of that now. In his last speech, he describes his life from the day the gentleman called to this moment as a failed attempt to put some distance between past and present, Laura and himself. He has always been pursued by guilt, the memory of his sister; it is what he tries to forget: "I reach for a cigarette, I cross the street, I run into the movies or a bar, I buy a drink, I speak to the nearest stranger—anything that can blow your candles out!" During the monologue, with the scrim being lowered, the play comes back on itself; Tom is left safely outside. On stage he has cast his memory in the form of a play, and the play succeeds where everything else failed. In the final scene, Laura stops her pursuit and takes her place in the past. A conjuring trick, the gentleman caller has shown Laura what Tom could never tell her: that her life is on the other side of the scrim which divides illusion and reality, in the dark. Though Tom has tried every other trick to blow the candles out, it is only Laura who can do that for him and only as a character in the play that she will. The final line of *The Glass Menagerie* is a stage direction.

*Tennessee Williams' Women: Illusion and Reality, Sexuality and Love

The critical labels commonly affixed to the women characters in the plays of Tennessee Williams are deceptively simple. Robert Jones

*By Jeanne M. McGlinn. From *Tennessee Williams: A Tribute,* edited by Jac Tharpe. Copyright© 1977 by the University Press of Mississippi, Jackson, Mississippi. Reprinted by permission from the University Press of Mississippi.

divides the "Early Heroines" into basically two types, the gentlewo-man of a genteel but mythical southern way of life and the sensual or natural woman. The gentlewoman cannot understand life in the modern world, and in her resultant alienation she seeks to recapture a way of life, the cavalier Old South, which never really existed. The sen-sual women are inhabitants of the New South and "seem to have been conceived by their creator, if not as representatives of a sort of salva-tion, then at least as attractive earth goddesses whose salvation is their own sexuality" ("Tennessee Williams' Early Heroines", p. 211). Jones considers sex as either a means of escape or a sign of liberation, depending on the woman's view of her own sexuality. John von Szeliski also feels the basic dramatic action of Williams' plays is sexual ("Tennessee Williams and the Tragedy of Sensitivity", p. 67). Critics agree on reading Williams' plays as sexual dramas in which the south-ern gentlewoman and the natural woman represent respectively the spirit and the flesh, though the sexual is the only creative and positive form of behavior. Yet a close reading of Williams' plays reveals a com-plexity in the women that makes these classifications incomplete.

In seven plays written in a twenty year period, Williams uses es-sentially the same dramatic situation. A woman is presented at a moment when frustration has led to a crisis. She has only two possible ways of acting: to face reality or to retreat into illusion. The significant question is whether she will face the crisis and choose to live in the real world, free of debilitating illusions and capable of compassion for others. Whatever value sex has for Williams, in some plays sexuality leads to illusion or is at least the result of a very self-centered view of reality. Neither situation is creative, whereas the ability to respond to the needs of another human being emerges as a higher value for Wil-liams. The human contact may be either physical or spiritual; what matters is the attempt to love—based on a realistic understanding of both oneself and another. Between 1940 and 1960 Williams moves from the delineation of women who live in illusion and hence are unable to love to the delineation of women who accept the reality of their lives and become concerned and compassionate or at least ready for unselfish love.

In two plays of the forties, *The Glass Menagerie* and *A Streetcar Named Desire,* the women characters all act under the influence of an illusionary view of both themselves and their world and so are unlov-ing. In *The Glass Menagerie,* both Amanda and Laura refuse to face the reality of their lives; Amanda retreats into the past, and Laura retreats into herself. Laura's withdrawal is more deadening than Amanda's, however, because she is completely self-centered. Amanada is at least trying to hold the family together, economically and spiritually. She tries to help Laura lead a normal life, first by send-ing her to business college then by making "plans and provisions" for a gentleman caller. These efforts for another human being, even

80

though undermined eventually by Amanda's illusions, corroborate Williams' description of Amanda as having "dignity and tragic beauty" (Vol I., p. 236, *The Theatre of Tennessee Williams*).

The crisis that led to Amanda's illusion came well before the play began. Her husband's desertion of her and the family was the shock that sent her back into the golden days of her girlhood. Since Amanda cannot face the reality that she was unable to hold her husband's love, she indulges in memories of that one supreme moment of her youth, the day when she might have chosen from seventeen gentleman callers, all rich and successful and caring for their wives. Williams describes Amanda as, "A little woman of great but confused vitality clinging frantically to another time and place," who "having failed to establish contact with reality, continues to live vitally in her illusions" (*ibid*, p. 129).

Removed into her past and needing to fortify an endangered sense of self-worth, Amanda assumes an archaic form of southern behavior, gentility. In the early American South a genteel code developed, giving the white southern woman homage both to safeguard her purity from the manhood of black slaves and to symbolize a civilizing influence on the decadent ways of the white landed gentry. (Cash, *The Mind of the South*, pp. 87-9). So "gentlemen callers" represent a time when men were chivalrous and women were respected, admired, and pampered. Amanda affects the pose of superiority granted by this code to women, along with the flirtatiousness of the genteel lady who could attract and allure, giving a man hopes of reward without committing herself.

Amanda can act as the southern belle, but when she tries to force the role on Laura, the result is a complete disintegration of Laura's personality. She has precariously managed to protect herself from what she regards as a harsh and judgmental world by making her own world out of old records and tiny glass figurines. Laura's retreat from the real world is a result of her belief that since she is crippled, she is unlovely and unloveable. Feeling unattractive, Laura is frightened by a situation in which this attractiveness is directly tested, entertaining a man. Her self-consciousness and introversion thus reach a climax during her evening with Jim, the gentleman caller.

Unable to act like Amanda, Laura eventually responds to Jim's warmth. She forgets herself as they talk and even trusts him with the unicorn, a symbol for herself. But after Jim kisses her and then apologizes because he is engaged, Laura immediately retreats for protection into her inner world: "She rises unsteadily and crouches beside the victrola to wind it up." Her distorted sense of reality prevents the realization that Jim's actions have nothing to do with her attractiveness. Self-centered for too long, she seems incapable of realizing that what comes into her world does not necessarily reflect on her. Given such a limited perception, Laura cannot participate in human relationships and will continue to be unhappy in the real world.

Blanche resembles both Amanda and Laura in her reactions to the harsh world. Her attempt to hold the crumbling world of the family plantation together is similar to Amanda's attempt to keep her family together. Also like Amanda, she refuses to accept the reality of her life and attempts to live under illusion. She has a false sense of gentility which is contradicted by an equally false flight to promiscuity. The conflict between these two modes of behavior means self-defeat instead of survival. At the play's end, Blanche can only retreat into an insanity that exceeds Laura's withdrawal.

Blanche's moment of crisis occurred when she discovered her husband was a homosexual and in a moment of disgust drove him to suicide. The memory recurs in vivid flashes to haunt Blanche who only wants to avoid the "blinding light." She does not want to face her rejection of her husband and the part she played in his suicide.

Criticism of Stella's sordid condition allows Blanche to forget her own unhappy life. She refuses to believe that Stella has adjusted to this new way of life which is so different from the plantation world where women were ladies. It is the "lady" that is speaking when Blanche judges Stanley, Stella's husband, as beneath them because he is not a gentleman. Blanche's attempt to maintain the image of herself as a correct and genteel lady also leads her to deny her real sexual nature. Blanche too pines for the "gentleman" who will rescue her.

Blanche's sexual nature asserts itself, however, contrary to her attempts at gentility, and this leads to her breakdown. She avoids adult sexual relationships but actively seeks affairs with adolescents. She has just been exiled from her hometown because she attempted to seduce a boy. She later admits that she has had many "one-night stands" with the young soldiers of the nearby army camp. And the stage action shows her urge to seduce a young newspaper boy. Blanche seeks relationships with boys both because she feels guilty about the death of her young husband and because she is sexually immature and inadequate. Though she does not wish for the complications of love, panic drives her to sex when her memories have made existence intolerable: "After the death of Allan—intimacies with strangers was all I seemed able to fill my empty heart with . . . I think it was panic, just panic, that drove me from one to another, hunting for some protection. . . ." After all, Blanche says, the opposite of death is desire.

Blanche's real motive for pursuing sexual relationships, however, seems to be the one she cannot face, her sexual inadequacy. Allan, she says, "came to me for help. I didn't know that . . . all I knew was I'd failed him in some mysterious way. . . ." It is this failure that Blanche is trying to exorcise by forming relationships with boys. She might be able to satisfy one of them in a way she was never able to satisfy her boyish husband Allan. This sense of inadequacy also accounts for her acute awareness of her physical attractiveness. She exercises her sexual charm to prove her allure—not for sexual gratification. Fearing that she will be unable to win a man and knowing that failure will mean that she will have to face herself, Blanche pursues Mitch. But she has no wish for a mature man-woman relationship and never really views Mitch as a sexual conquest. Blanche's feelings for Mitch are totally self-centered. She sees him as "a cleft in the rock of the world that I could hide in!" She wants him to protect her from her persistent vision of Allan's suicide: "You've stopped that polka tune that I had caught in my head."

Stanley, in his ignorance and insensitivity, destroys both Blanche's hope and her illusion. He sees through her pose without understanding why she needs one. He thinks merely that she feels superior to him, and he wishes to destroy her composure to make her recognize that she is the same as he, a sexual animal. Stanley takes Blanche's teasing as a sign of real sexuality and concludes that they've "had this date with each other from the beginning!" The rape shatters Blanche's desperate pose for dignity and also forces on her what she is inadequate to endure, raw sexual passion. The result is insanity.

Blanche's sister, Stella, deals with reality in a basically healthy way. Rather than holding on to the old way of life at Belle Reve, she left to make her own living. Survival is always self-centered, however, as Blanche knows when she accuses Stella of deserting the family. Stella ignores the needs of others and eventually adopts her own illusion. Life with Stanley—sex with Stanley—is her highest value. Her refusal to accept Blanche's story of the rape is a commitment to self-preservation rather than love, and thus Stella contributes to Blanche's disintegration.

In *Summer and Smoke* written in 1948 Williams' characterization of women begins to change. Alma, unlike the heroines of the early plays who reject reality, develops in the course of the play from a woman who lives in the illusion of impossible aspiration and idealism into a woman who accepts reality and who actively seeks what she wants. Concurrent with this development, she grows in her capability to communicate with others. She overcomes her egocentrism and self-pity and offers kindness to someone in need.

The crisis that leads to this change in Alma is her complex feelings about herself and her life during this summer of her middle twenties. She feels that her youth is passing and knows that she is already considered an old maid. She resents the need to care for a senile and selfish mother and a self-pitying father: "I have had certain difficulties and disadvantages to cope with—which may be partly the cause of these peculiarities of mine. . . ." Then John Buchanan, the boy whom Alma has always loved, returns and disturbs Alma with his rejection of her idealism and his insistence on the physical nature of relationships between a man and a woman.

Highly idealistic behavior has always come naturally to Alma since she is the daughter of a minister. Even as a ten-year-old child she was adultlike, dignified with a quality of spirituality, and intrigued by the idea of eternity. These characteristics have intensified with age. The playwright says, "An excessive propriety and self-consciousness is apparent in her nervous laughter. . . ." Alma's day-dreams about eternity have solidified into a philosophy of other-worldliness. The symbol of her idealism is the Gothic cathedral because "everything seems to be straining for something out of the reach of stone—or human—fingers." Life, to Alma, is "the everlasting struggle and aspiration for more than our human limits have placed in our reach." Man lives in the gutter, she believes, but "some of us are looking at the stars."

This idealism is illusionary, however, because Alma has been unable to translate it into positive action. Her care of her mother leads her to self-pity. She is bitter because she has not gotten anything for her sacrifice, not even recognition. Her life tied to duty, Alma has a dream about what she would do if things were different. She says to John, "Most of us have no choice but to lead useless lives! But you . . . have a chance to serve humanity. Not just to go on enduring for the sake of endurance, but to serve a noble, humanitarian cause, to relieve human suffering."

Alma also has an exalted notion of the role of woman as a wife and mother. She thinks a woman must bring her heart and her soul to marriage, and she rejects sexuality as often no better than bestiality. She rejects John's anatomy lesson: "I reject your opinion of where love is, and the kind of truth you believe the brain to be seeking!— There is something not shown on the chart." Alma, of course, means the soul. John sees this ideal as another example of Alma's Gothic cathedral image of life and suggests that Alma would never be satisfied with a normal love relationship; she would be striving for the impossible. Alma admits that her attempts to establish relationships with men have all failed because of "a desert between us." She has never been able to care for any man: "None of them really engaged my serious feelings." The one man Alma loves, John, she has loved with her soul, but he rejects this love. It is, he tells her, actually what kept him away from her: "The night at the casino—I wouldn't have made love to you . . . I'm more afraid of your soul than you're afraid of my body. You'd have been as safe as the angel of the fountain—because I wouldn't feel *decent* enough to touch you. . . ."

With the impact of her whole situation and with John's rejection, Alma is forced to see that her idealism does not lead to positive acts in her own life. After a period of physical collapse and mental turmoil, she decides to pursue personal fulfilment. She decides that a person "can ask for the coming true of his most impossible dreams." Her old self is dead: "the girl who said 'no,' she doesn't exist any more." Though Alma realizes that she can no longer marry John, she reveals her new strength when she goes to him to declare that she loves him: "I haven't come here on any but equal terms. . . . It's no longer a secret that I love you. It never was." She does not indulge in self-pity. She attempts to understand what has happened to her former relationship with John and, unselfishly, hides her tears rather than detract from Nellie's happiness.

In the last scene, Alma is administering to a lonely and nervous traveling salesman. She has lost her extreme propriety; she laughs naturally and engages in light banter. Unencumbered by a false ideal of what love should be, she is ready to accept another for what he is and make the most of this human contact. This may not be a relationship "to engage her serious feelings," but it is a relationship that springs from a new genuineness and a clearer view of reality. In earlier plays women were able to find relief from emotional crises only in illusion, but in *Summer and Smoke* and the subsequent plays of the fifties except for *Orpheus Descending* Williams portrays women able to face reality and enjoy healthier relationships.

In *The Rose Tattoo,* Williams depicts Serafina, who with a "woman's heart passionately in love," idealizes her marriage with Rosario. To her, married sex is the ultimate experience, "a religion," and she is proud of her adherence to its values: faithfulness, chastity, and purity. But the idea that making love had consecrated her and her husband is an illusion because Rosario was not faithful, and there is no indication that he even loved Serafina. After his death, she continues to exalt his memory and maintains her idealization of their relationship. In order to do this, she cloisters herself from the real world. Putting her "heart in the marble urn with the ashes," she quits taking care of herself, lives in the past, and talks to the ashes.

When Serafina learns after years of homage that Rosario defiled their marriage bed, she is freed from her illusion. She does not react as Amanda does to her husband's desertion. Instead the truth frees Serafina from adoration of a memory. She is saved from despair by Alvaro to whom she turns in a relationship so practical that it cannot be idealized. He admits the economic advantages of marriage with Serafina, but at the same time he offers "Love and affection!—in a world that is lonely—and cold!" Serafina comes through her crisis to realize, like Alma, that life is too important to reject for a memory.

Unlike Serafina, Maggie of *Cat on a Hot Tin Roof* has no illusions at the time of the play. Instead she is clear about her two main goals: to acquire money and to overcome her estrangement from Brick. She says she wants money so she can take care of Brick, and she refuses to leave him because she loves him. It is difficult to believe her motivation is other-centered, however, because of information which indicates how selfishly she acted in her earlier days. She forced Brick to marry her; and then when she saw Skipper as a threat to her relationship with Brick, she accused him of homosexuality even though she knew it would be devastating to him. She admits she acted wrongly since she now knows Brick desires only the most ideal relationship. Her self-centeredness has caused her to act in illusion.

Maggie is motivated in part by a background of genteel poverty. Growing up, she felt inferior because her family had to struggle to maintain a respectable standard of living despite an alcoholic father. Maggie resented the rich relatives who expected her fondest gratitude in exchange for castoff possessions. Now she says she must have money to feel good in old age.

The effect of this information is to make all her actions ambiguous. When she manipulates everyone around her in her competition with Mae and Gooper for Big Daddy's estate, she may only want the money for herself. On the other hand, she may be acting out of love for Brick, as she says. No matter for what reasons, when she uses Brick's alcoholism to accomplish her ends, her actions can only appear destructive. This ambiguity is compounded because whatever Maggie does for her husband, she ultimately does for herself as well. Securing an inheritance will benefit them both. An emotionally whole Brick will be a better lover for Maggie.

Two elements of the play, Maggie's identification with Big Mama and the revised act three, indicate the author's intention and resolve our questions. Big Mama and Maggie have similar relationships with their husbands. Both love the same type of man; Big Daddy is just an older version of Brick. Williams says he "must have had something Brick has, who made himself loved so much by the 'simple expedient' of not loving enough to disturb his charming detachment, also once coupled, like Brick's, with virile beauty" (Vol. III, p. 138-39 *Theatre*). And both women are misunderstood by their husbands who find it hard to believe in their love. When their wives declare their love, both men respond with the same words, "Wouldn't it be funny if that was true?" Big Mama's joy that Daddy will live, her anguish when she learns the truth, her refusal to let the children appropriate his power, and her hurt when she sees that Big Daddy does not know how much she loves him all demonstrate that she loves unselfishly. By identifying Maggie with Mama, Williams shows he thinks Maggie is a lover too.

The revision of the third act further explains Maggie's character. Elia Kazan influenced the changes to show a Maggie who is less ambiguous in her actions because he wanted her character to be "more clearly sympathetic to an audience." Williams accepted this suggestion "wholeheartedly" because Maggie "had become steadily more charming to me as I worked on her characterization." (*ibid*, p. 168). As a result, the Maggie that emerges is no longer as manipulative or destructive to others.

Maggie seems genuinely concerned about Big Mama when she calls Brick to comfort her. Whereas in the original play Maggie called Brick only at Mama's bidding, several lines of dialogue have been added to show that Maggie anticipates Big Mama's need for comfort and support against Mae and Gooper and their plans. She says to Brick, "they're going to tell Big Mama the truth now, an' she needs you!" Maggie even uses a threat: "I'm going to take every dam' bottle on this place an' pitch it off th' levee into th' river!"—to make Brick respond. In the original, when Maggie used this threat, she was manipulating a helpless man. Here Brick is strong enough that he is not threatened and hears her words as a sign of vitality and determination.

The other major change in the action grows from Brick's self-realization. In the Broadway version the change in Brick's awareness of his guilt is immediate, and so he is less defensive towards Maggie. He is able to respect her vitality and he accepts her aid. When Maggie maneuvers to defeat the ambitions of Mae and Gooper with news of her pregnancy, Brick gives her support. The revised last scene also suggests that Brick responds with love to Maggie. Encountering the thoroughness of her determination, he does not abjectly give up with nothing to say. Rather, he says, "I admire you, Maggie." The stage action shows his willingness to turn out the lights and begin their love-making. His receptiveness makes Maggie's final speech ring true: "Oh, you weak, beautiful people who give up with such grace. What you need is someone to take hold of you—gently, with love, and hand your life back to you . . . and I can! I'm determined to do it. . . ." Maggie is a vital woman who can be misunderstood, but the weight of the play tends to move our understanding of her as a person who, if responsive to her own needs, is at least equally responsive to the needs of other persons around her.

Unlike Maggie, the women in *Orpheus Descending* are so involved in trying to survive in a hostile and violent society that they have not strength left for healthy relationships. Vee Talbot, the sheriff's wife, faces the cruelty and violence of the county jail. She sees "awful things take place:" beatings, lynchings, runaway convicts torn to pieces by dogs. Moral corruption marks the society which spawns such violence. The women are backbiters and adulterers; the men are intolerant and sadistic.

Vee believes she has a mission to help people, to "save" them, to "build up characters!" but the townspeople scorn her religiosity. Confused by the world of light and shadow, religion and hatred, which she inhabits, Vee turns to her paintings as a method of survival. Denying the appearances of the world as misleading, she believes visions are the only way to see and so paints under their influence. Val articulates her feelings about her art best when he says, "You make some beauty out of this dark country." Her creativity leaves her exhausted but elevated above and purified of the gross world. Her paintings are an escape into fantasy which eventually blind her totally to the real world.

Carol, a member of an aristocratic family in the town, tried to struggle singlehandedly against its cruelty and injustice. She delivered speeches, wrote letters, and protested against the injustices done to the black people by the white minority. She says, "I thought it was wrong for pellagra and slow starvation to cut them down when the cotton crop failed from army worm or boll weevil or too much rain in summer." So she used her inheritance to set up free clinics. Then when a black man was electrocuted "for having improper relations with a white whore," she personally protested by setting off for the capital, on foot in winter, dressed in a potato sack. The reaction of the town was to hoot, jeer, spit at her and arrest her for lewd vagrancy.

Her economic resources bankrupt and her personal sense of well-being threatened by the rejection of her family and community, Carol employs bizarre survival tactics. Having people talk about her is one way of knowing she is alive, and so she irritates the populace: "I want to be noticed, seen, heard, felt! I want them to know I'm alive!" Movement gives her a sense of life so her life now is the endless, restless round of "jooking," driving, drinking, dancing, and lovemaking. She uses sex, even though it is painful and potentially dangerous, just "to be not alone, even for a few moments." Because she sees contact with another person as a way to feel alive, Carol's idea of a relationship is holding onto another for all she's worth. She says, "What on earth can you do on this earth but catch at whatever comes near you, with both your hands, until your fingers are broken?" Carol is too threatened to be able to forget herself and love another for his own sake.

Lady also lives with the effects of small town hatred and intolerance. Her father was burned to death in the fire set to teach him a lesson because "he sold liquor to niggers." Then Lady was rejected by her lover for a woman with social status and wealth. Badly hurt, she gave up on life and "sold" herself to a loveless marriage. Yet, she believes life has some meaning. She tells Val there is more to life than corruption, because "If I thought that was the answer I'd take Jabe's pistol or his morphine tablets." Lady does not want to die, and so she tries to begin living again. She wants to open a replica of her father's wine garden in the confectionery of the Torrence store. In this way, she will reassert her father's presence and her own identity in the face of the town's resistance. She hopes to overcome David's rejection and regain self-esteem by reviving the richness of the time when he loved her. She tells him, "don't pity me . . . in there's the confectionery which'll reopen this spring, . . . it's going to be like—the wine garden of my father, those wine-drinking nights when you had something better than anything you've had since!" When Lady learns that Jabe was the leader of the Mystic Crew the night her father was burned out, the revival becomes "necessary, it's just something's got to be done to square things away. . . . *Just to be not defeated!*"

This single ambition to endure consumes Lady. She will use any means to obtain her end, including Val. She begs him to stay with her, not because she loves him but because she needs him "TO LIVE . . . TO GO ON LIVING!!!" When the situation in the town threatens him and he wants to leave, Lady selfishly keeps him with her, promising that they will go after she has had her revenge. Then when she realizes she is pregnant, Lady does not need Val anymore and tells him to leave. She has life now and is self-sustaining. It seems an inconsistency when she covers Val with her body and takes her husband's bullets. This self-sacrificing behavior is out of line with her pattern of survival.

None of the women in *Orpheus Descending* achieves even the readiness for compassionate love. A sense of acceptance of and survival in the real world must come first. Williams' characters in the Fifties generally attain these qualities. This play is an exception possibly because it is a reworking of a play of 1940, *Battle of Angels*.

In *The Night of the Iguana,* Williams repeats in the character of Hannah Jelkes the basic theme that facing reality may develop compassion. Williams says, "She suggests a Gothic cathedral image of a medieval saint, but animated . . . she is totally feminine and yet androgynous-looking—almost timeless" (Vol. IV, p. 266, *Theatre*). Hannah's femininity takes the form of the comforting mother figure, as Shannon perhaps realizes when he calls her "Miss . . . Thin-Standing-Up-Female-Buddha." She does, in any case immediately respond to Shannon's obvious need for compassion.

Hannah is compassionate because she has endured her own personal crisis and is able to sympathize with the confusion and panic of others. She tells Shannon: "I can help you because I've been through what you are going through now. . . . I showed (my spook) that I could endure him and I make him respect my endurance." Hannah has saved herself from passive existence in a dream world by controlling her panic: "I never cracked up, I couldn't afford to. . . . My work, this occupational therapy that I gave myself—painting and doing quick character sketches—made me look out of myself, not in, and gradually, at the far end of the tunnel that I was struggling out of I began to see this faint, very faint grey light—the light of the world outside me—and I kept climbing toward it." The experience has made her feel that people need "A little understanding exchanged between them, a wanting to help each other through nights like this." Despite her own immediate problems with her grandfather's illness and their penury, Hannah acts on her belief that people can "see and know each other" and "if they're decent . . . help each other all that they can."

Hannah's kindness contrasts with the sensual egocentrism of Maxine, "a stout, swarthy woman in her middle forties—affable and rapaciously lusty." She demands male attention and seeks it from Shannon as well as the Mexican boys. Maxine thinks she has no illusions. She says to Shannon, "I know the difference between loving someone and just sleeping with someone—even I know about that. We've both reached a point where we've got to settle for something that works for us in our lives—even if it isn't on the highest kind of level." However, her willingness to substitute immediate gratification for human contact and creative love make her weaker than Hannah who always seeks the human contact. In fact, Maxine's sexual drives lead to her false assessment of the relationship between Hannah and Shannon as sexual. "I got the vibrations between you. . . ," she says, "and there sure was a vibration between you and Shannon the moment you got here. That, just that, believe me, nothing but that has made this . . . misunderstanding between us." As a result, Maxine wants to send Hannah and her grandfather, who is hardly able to travel, away from the hotel. Maxine's sexual drives make her selfish, deluded, and unkind.

Examination of Williams' women characters shows that over-simplified classifications are inadequate. Williams gradually charac-terized women to dramatize the theme that a woman must avoid illusions about both herself and others. Amanda is too involved in illu-sion to see her daughter's mental condition, and Laura is too involved in self to love. Blanche has failed once at love and spends the rest of her life trying to avoid it. Stella's sexuality leads her to choose illusion and life with Stanley rather than truth and love for Blanche. Later, women face reality and so acquire the capacity to be loving. Alma is saved from lovelessness by the realization that her false idealism pre-vents her from making real contact with others. Serafina is on the way to a healthier relationship when she realizes she has over-idealized mar-ried sex and withdrawn from life. Maggie is so vital that she is not subject to illusion for long, and she eventually attains unselfish behavior.

In all these plays, sexuality has been present but not necessarily the primary ingredient in the relationships. In *The Night of the Iguana* Williams makes a clear statement that sexuality is not a necessary pre-requisite to a loving relationship. Hannah is not sexual, but she is totally selfless and responsive to the needs of others. On the other hand, Maxine's sexuality makes her self-centered. Clearly, Williams indicates the independence of human compassion from human sexual-ity and, more importantly, the interdependence of love and under-standing. The women who idealize reality retreat into an illusionary world. They use bizarre behavior because they cannot accept them-selves or others. Women who face reality are in the middle ground, committed to the here and now, and vital. Their desire to live may eventually be selfish or loving. The women who are realists and who sympathize with others and their problems are the truly compassion-ate. Williams has called himself an old romanticist. Judging by the plays considered, by "romanticist" he must mean one who believes in the power of love; and the fullest love, as Williams shows, is compas-sion formed only in reality.

Bibliography

Brooks, Charles B. "The Comic Tennessee Williams," *The Quarterly Journal of Speech,* 44 (October 1958), 275-81.

Cash, W.J. *The Mind of the South.* New York: Random House, Vintage, 1941.

Debusscher, Gilbert. "Tennessee Williams' Unicorn Broken Again." *Revue belge de Philologie et d'Histoire* Brussels), 49 (1971), 875-85. Discussion of *The Glass Menagerie.*

Durham, Frank. "Tennessee Williams: Theatre Poet in Prose." *South Atlantic Bulletin,* 36 (March 1971), 3-16. Discussion of *The Glass Menagerie.*

Falk, Signi Lenea. *Tennessee Williams.* New York: Twayne, 1961.

Fritscher, John J. "Some Attitudes and a Posture: Religious Metaphor and Ritual in Tennessee Williams' Query of God." *Modern Drama,* 13 (September 1970).

Hughes, Catharine R. *Tennessee Williams: A Biography.* Englewood Cliffs, N.J.: Prentice-Hall, Inc., 1978.

Jackson, Esther Merle. "Tennessee Williams." In *The American Theater Today,* edited by Alan S. Downer, pp. 73-84. New York: Basic Books, Inc., 1967.

Jones, Robert. "Tennessee Williams' Early Heroines." *Modern Drama,* 2 (1959), 211-219.

Kahn, Sy M. "Through a Glass Menagerie Darkly: The World of Tennessee Williams." In *Modern American Drama: Essays in Criticism,* edited by William E. Taylor, Deland, Florida: Everett/ Edwards, 1968.

King, Thomas L. "Irony and Distance in *The Glass Menagerie.*" *Educational Theatre Journal,* 25 (May 1973). 207-14.

Miller, Jordan Y., ed. *Twentieth Century Interpretations of A Streetcar Named Desire.* Englewood Cliffs, N.J.: Prentice-Hall Inc., 1971.

Nelson, Benjamin. *Tennessee Williams: The Man and His Work.* New York: Ivan Obolensky, 1961.

Tharpe, Jac L., ed. *Tennessee Williams: A Tribute.* Jackson: University Press of Mississippi, 1977. A volume of critical essays.

Tischler, Nancy M. *Tennessee Williams: Rebellious Puritan.* New York: Citadel Press, 1961.

Von Szeliski, John. "Tennessee Williams and the Tragedy of Sensitivity." *Twentieth Century Interpretations of a Streetcar Named Desire.*

Weales, Gerald. *Tennessee Williams.* Minneapolis: University of Minnesota Press. 1965.

Weissman, Philip. "A Trio of Tennessee Williams' Heroines: The Psychology of Prostitution." In *Creativity in the Theater.* New York: Basic Books, Inc., 1965.

Williams, Tennessee. *The Theatre of Tennessee Williams.* Five Volumes. New York: New Directions, 1971-1976.